COME APART
AND
REST FOR A WHILE

To all my Franciscan Minoress Sisters
and
visiting guest-hermits to the Portiuncula

COME APART
AND
REST FOR A WHILE

Patricia Jordan, FSM

GRACEWING

First published in 2008

Gracewing
2 Southern Avenue
Leominster
Herefordshire HR6 0QF

ISBN 978 0 85244 691 1

Typeset by Action Publishing Technology Ltd, Gloucester GL1 5SR

Printed by
Cambrian Printers, Aberystwyth SY23 3TN

CONTENTS

FOREWORD

In our modern age there are few opportunities to stand aside from our busy lives and reflect on God's relationship with us. At the heart of the Franciscan vocation is a place of solitude. It is there that the encounter with God takes place and our response is determined.

The Franciscan Minoress Sisters have overcome many challenges to establish the Portiuncula at Clay Cross in Derbyshire to provide the hermitage experience for those who can avail themselves of this wonderful facility. Sister Patricia Jordan has captured the spirit of the place in this book. She invites you to 'come apart and rest for a while' as you are led through the reflections and devotions in St Francis' company. Through these pages you will come to a clearer knowledge of God and gain a greater knowledge of his many blessings.

Malcolm McMahon, OP
Bishop of Nottingham

PREFACE

The Portiuncula of St Francis' time lies about three kilometres southwest of Assisi and is protected within the beautiful Basilica of Santa Maria degli Angeli. It was there in the tiny chapel of the Portiuncula that St Francis received his call from God on the Feast of St Matthias 1209 when the Gospel reading at Mass included the words, 'Take no gold, silver, or copper in your belts, no pack for the road, no second coat, no sandals, no stick; the worker deserves his keep.' St Francis interpreted this as a call to embrace personal poverty. The Portiuncula became a special place in the Order St Francis founded and his brethren met there for their chapter meetings.

The poverty characteristic of the Franciscans emphasized the wonder of the rest of creation and of God's love. Hence St Francis' passionate hymn rejoicing in all aspects of creation. All are manifestations of God's creative love. He had a particular devotion to the infant Jesus, the manifestation of God's love in the poverty of Bethlehem. He is the first to use models of the crib to illustrate his popular preaching, with Jesus the Son of God lying in the manger. Similarly, the simplicity of the Eucharist, where Jesus makes himself present in the form of bread and wine demonstrates how he makes himself available to all as manifestations of God's love.

St Francis set out on a life of evangelization through preaching and demonstrating his poverty, but this practical work was always rooted in prayer. Like Jesus, he withdrew regularly for prayer. He wrote a *Rule for Hermitages*, but even here there was an element of brotherhood, for the hermits were expected to retreat in groups of about four, where two of the group would provide for the needs of the others.

When the Franciscan Minoress Sisters decided to build a centre for prayer and solitude at their convent of St Clare in Clay Cross in Derbyshire, they called it the Portiuncula, to echo the significance of St Francis' Portiuncula in Assisi. That was one of the places where St Francis and his brethren met to experience anew the unconditional love of God, to renew their sense of God's call and to gain renewed strength for their evangelical work. It would serve the same purpose in the modern world, where people could come to experience anew God's personal love and renew their sense of purpose in whatever God had called them to do. The architecture of the centre reflects this.

The Portiuncula at the Franciscan convent in Derbyshire, for which Sr Patricia Jordan has done the background research and advised on the design and construction, is a remarkable achievement as well as a beautiful building. The individual hermitages lead through to the chapel, and are grouped so that individuals are aware of a community of like-minded participants. It provides people with the opportunity and facilities for the hermitage experience, which had such a prominent place in St Francis' own life. Sr Patricia's book shows just how St Francis planned and achieved this, and how important and valuable it still is. The Franciscan hermitage pattern has now been made practicable for retreatants, whether religious or lay, and this book by Sister Patricia makes it all the more accessible to them.

The design of the hermitage is the outcome of several years of research by Sister Patricia into the influence of the Bible – both the Old and New Testaments – and the teachings of the Church Fathers on St Francis' own thinking as shown in his writings. This research programme earned her both a doctorate and a university prize.

Come Apart and Rest for a While is a very readable book, primarily for people staying at the hermitage, but also applicable to people in their own homes. It is a powerful devotional work, written in the first person as if by St Francis himself, which I personally found very moving when I first read it.

Dr Joseph Rhymer, BA, M.Th., Th.D.

ACKNOWLEDGEMENTS

I am deeply grateful to Sister Columba, my Superior General and to my Congregation for supporting the Portiuncula project in its written and architectural expression. My own community of sisters at St Clare's deserve a special 'Thank You' for their on-going prayer, support, help and encouragement and to Sister Dorothy Paul for her generous self-giving and expertise in computer skills and digital photography. Sister Anthony deserves special mention for the beauty created by her gifted artistic work throughout the Portiuncula and Peace Garden. The building of the Portiuncula and the publication of two books associated with it – the first *An Affair of the Heart* and this companion volume *Come Apart and Rest for a While* – has been a community and congregational adventure in faith.

Special thanks are due to Dominic Williams from Ellis-Williams Architects and to his design team for their sensitive, skilful and empathetic interpretation of our vision for the Portiuncula.

Thanks go to Bosco Construction, especially the Directors, Bruno Quiligotti and Paul Marsh, for accepting this contract with great confidence and optimism. We extend our special thanks and appreciation to Mike Murray and all those too numerous to mention, but all appreciated, who have worked with him on site.

To Bowmer and Kirkland Property Services Limited for their dedicated undertaking of the Completion Works. Peter Hawkins and his team deserve special mention for their competence, co-operation and sensitivity in making our vision a reality.

To Alan Arnott of Studio Nine for Lighting; to Scobie Alvis of Faber Maunsell for Structural Engineering; to David Hibbert and Richard Trench of Goth Hibbert for Quantity Surveying; to Cate Watkinson for her original and inspirational interpretation of the Canticle of St Francis in stained glass; to Ram Roof for supplying a beautiful and ecologically friendly 'Green Roof'; to Real Stone for their donation of a stone fountain and their expertise in creating a real 'hermitage' expression, modelled on the Portiuncula hermitage in Assisi: thank you to them all.

Finally, I wish to express my deep gratitude to Tom Longford from Gracewing Publishers and to Jo Whale for her encouragement and patient working with me through the manuscript to bring the text to its present book form.

To so many people, named and unnamed, I commend each and all to the heart of God in deep gratitude and appreciation.

INTRODUCTION

This little book was written as a companion book to *An Affair of the Heart* and it is offered as a prayerful guide for a time 'set apart'. Though the focus is the Portiuncula in rural Derbyshire in England, the spirit is that of the Portiuncula in Assisi. Yet, even in saying that, there is another dimension that transcends time and place. It is that moment of encounter and surrender that often happens in the time set apart for the Lord. It is that moment experienced in the depths of the heart when the love of God invites, purifies, embraces, holds us and finally overwhelms us. In his Letter to the Philippians (3:12) St Paul says, 'Christ Jesus took hold of me,' and in his Letter to the Corinthians, he says, 'the love of Christ overwhelms us …' (2 Cor. 5:14).

Saint Francis experienced the agony and the ecstasy that often permeates times intentionally set apart for solitude. He entered the sacred space that belongs to God alone, the place where we are called by name and where we grow in our understanding of our identity in Christ Jesus. It is a sacred place and a sacred moment on the heart's journey into God. That sacred place is your own heart but it has long been recognized that an exterior place apart may facilitate the encounter with God and the surrender to God.

Under the inspiring leadership of Fr Roch Niemier, OFM, Fr Murray Bodo, OFM, and the late Fr Aaron Pembleton, OFM, I have had the privilege of spending a month in Assisi and the surrounding areas where St Francis spent time in solitude. I have tried to capture the spirit of those places and the graces associated with them that you too may be helped on your journey into the mystery of God's love in the depths of your heart. You may not be able to visit the actual places in Assisi or the Portiuncula in Derbyshire but be inspired and consoled as you remember that wherever you are, the dwelling place of God is within your own heart and there is a timeless relevance to these precious words of St Francis:

> Brother Body is our cell, and our soul is the hermit
> that dwells within it, to pray to God and to meditate.
> If the soul does not live in peace and solitude in its cell,
> a cell made by hands profits a religious little.[1]

---

[1] Armstrong *et al*, *Francis of Assisi*, vol. 2, p. 215.

THE PORTIUNCULA

Most people have a favourite place, or favourite places to which they like to return. I would like to tell you about my favourite place, one that I loved more than any other place on earth. But first let me introduce myself. My name is Francesco Bernardone, more widely known now as St Francis of Assisi and I  want to welcome you to Our Lady of the Angels of the Portiuncula, in rural Derbyshire, England. Together let us prayerfully experience this sacred space and enter into its symbolism and spirituality. Let us desire to draw near to the heart of our God in the presence of Mary our Mother and a host of angels who frequent this holy place.

ASSISI PORTIUNCULA

To begin, I must tell you that the Portiuncula in Assisi has a long history and I am so pleased that its message and spirit continue to touch the hearts of so many people in so many parts of our world today. It will always be so. To visit the Portiuncula is to journey to the heart of our gospel gift, expressed in so many wondrous ways

through so many different people. The Portiuncula — whether in Assisi, in Derbyshire, or in the depths of your own heart — is the place of God's special visitation. It is the dwelling place of God and his blessed Mother.

In the presence of Our Lady and the holy angels, I still associate the Portiuncula with birth, discovery, decision, mission, pardon and peace. There I came to birth as a Gospel person, walking in the footprints of Jesus whom I discovered in the living words of sacred Scripture. There in that little chapel in Assisi, my heart burned within me as I discovered my vocation in the Word of God and I exclaimed:

> This is what I want; this is what I seek; this is what I desire with all my heart.[1]

I hope that you too will be able to voice these same sentiments as you open your heart to the living words of the Gospel. Of course, for me, it was not just a personal re-birth; it never is! Gradually you will realize that your personal vocation is never for yourself alone. You will experience a sense of mission to share that which you have been given so generously. God in his mercy has called us not for our own good alone but for good of many.

Soon the Lord gave me brothers and sisters who thirsted as I did for the gospel message of love, forgiveness, peace and joy. All we needed to do was to open our hearts and surrender our lives to the Lord of love, trusting in divine providence that feeds the birds of the air and clothes the lilies of the fields. This gospel lesson we learned very quickly at the Portiuncula where we lived our lives of prayer and service in simplicity and joy.

As our spiritual family grew, the brothers went out two by two, from the Portiuncula, to many different parts of the world to share our gospel gift and proclaim the love of God to all our brothers and sisters.

OUR BROTHER LEPERS

We were especially tender towards the lepers, the poor and the excluded. There we recognized the suffering Christ and deemed it a privilege to tend him in whatever way he disguised himself. I think the Jesus of the Gospels likes to disguise himself. We have only to think of the resurrection stories where he presents himself as a gardener, as a traveller, as a cook and as a fisherman. Did he not promise: 'I will be with you always, yes, until the end of time.' Somehow, the Portiuncula intensifies this presence. So let the journey begin.

THE TRINITY GATE

In sacred Scripture 'gate' is used in many different ways in our relationship with God. You will get used to me quoting sacred Scripture. I have always loved the living word of God. There I found my heart's desire as God revealed his holy will to me. You too, will experience this as you open yourself to this experience. Now, at the beginning of our journey, the gate in Scripture is symbolically presented as a point of both strength and weakness. The Book of Genesis[2] tells us that to possess the gate is to conquer and so it is a position of strength. I like to think that passing through this gate to spend time apart with the Lord will also help you to conquer whatever keeps you from entering into a deeper relationship with him.

The Book of Genesis[3] also speaks of the enemy at the gate. It is good to be vigilant and seeing this gate is a reminder of that truth. The Psalms,[4] the prophets[5] and the evangelists[6] give us the beautiful image of the Gate as the entrance to heaven and holiness. Let us pray that this gate will be for you the Gate of the Lord,[7] the entrance to a holy place where God is waiting for you.

THE TRINITY SYMBOL

In the centre of the gate there is a circle in gold within which are three interlocking shapes in blue, red and green. This symbol for the Trinity dates back to AD 186 to Bishop Theophile of Antioch. Sometimes it is referred to as the Celtic symbol for the Trinity. The gold circle represents the Godhead and the unity of God. The three interlocking shapes represent the three Persons within the Trinity: the Father, the Son and the Holy Spirit. The symbol of the Trinity is there as a reminder of the invitation to share in the life and love of the community of the Trinity. To open the Trinity Gate is to respond to Love's beckoning and continue the journey to deeper intimacy with the Father, the Son and the Holy Spirit.

THE PATH

In Scripture the theme of journey is a very familiar one. As we walk, let us ponder on the theme of journey – your own personal journey. You may wish to reflect on the stepping stones on your journey through life and the many people who have touched your life's journey so far. You will remember the two disciples on their journey to Emmaus in St Luke's Gospel.[8] In the course of their journey, St Luke tells us that Jesus came up and walked by their side. I pray that you too will experience the real presence of Jesus as your companion on this journey. Usually when we set out on a journey we follow a particular path or way. My dear friend, Clare of Assisi and myself were deeply comforted by the assurance of Jesus' words: 'I am the Way'.[9] With Jesus as our Way, we have no need to fear because we also have the assurance that he is our light and our guide as we journey.[10]

PATH LIGHTS

As you walk with Jesus, notice the lights that are set into the path and listen to those comforting words: 'I am the light of the world; anyone who follows me will not be walking in the dark; he will have the light of life.'[11] Talk to Jesus the light of the world in your own words. Give thanks for all the expressions of light you see around you. Ask God to enlighten your heart so that you may know his great love for you.

Having the lights in the earth is also a reminder that we too have the light of Christ within us, in our earthliness. What an awesome reality it is when we begin to realize our dignity. I remember writing about this to the brothers, saying:

> Consider, O human being, in what great excellence the Lord God has placed you, for He created and formed you *to the image* of His beloved Son according to the body and *to His likeness* according to the Spirit.[12]

MARY OUR MOTHER

Let us pause now as we approach Mary our Mother who, with arms outstretched lovingly and warmly welcomes you to the Portiuncula. Jesus desires that you take to heart and cherish the precious gift he gave you from the Cross: 'This is your Mother.'

THE CROSS

As we draw nearer to the Portiuncula, let us look at the large cross on the chapel and pray those words I taught my companions so long ago, whenever we saw a cross: We adore You, Lord Jesus Christ, in all Your churches throughout the whole world and we bless You because by Your holy cross You have redeemed the world.[13]

STONES

I remember so well rebuilding with my own hands that little dilapidated church of the Portiuncula in Assisi. I collected the stones myself from my Assisi, and I see that this Portiuncula in rural Derbyshire is also made with local stone. That pleases me. Stones have always spoken to my heart because of Jesus, the living stone. Let us listen to those lovely and living words of sacred Scripture.

> He is the living stone, rejected by human beings
> but chosen by God and precious to him;
> set yourselves close to him so that you, too,
> may be living stones making a spiritual house.[14]

> Yahweh is my rock and my fortress,
> my deliverer is my God.
> I take refuge in him, my rock,
> my shield, my saving strength,
> my stronghold, my place of refuge.[15]

TEARS OF LOVE

But let us continue our journey. Did you notice the invitation to become stones making a spiritual building? Yes, if only the world realized that we are all sisters and brothers. These very stones speak to me of our union with each other and the love that binds us together. St Paul tells us this so eloquently when he says: 'Christ Jesus himself is the foundation stone. In him the whole building is bonded together and grows into a holy temple in the Lord. In him you too are being built with all the rest into a spiritual dwelling for God.'[16] Love is the whole of the Gospel Message and I still weep that Love is not loved.

THE SEDUM ROOF

Creation has always been a way to God for me and I was very aware of my responsibility to care for, and reverence the gift of creation. This aspect of my life has not gone unnoticed and Pope John Paul II named me the Patron Saint of Ecology. You too will grow in your understanding of the beautiful inter-relatedness we have with the whole of created reality. Friar Bonaventure reflecting on my relationship with creation, wrote this about me:

Aroused by everything to divine love, he rejoiced in all the works of the Lord's hands and through their delightful display he rose into their life-giving reason and cause. In beautiful things he contuited Beauty itself and through the footprints impressed in things he followed his Beloved everywhere, out of them all making for himself a ladder through which he could climb up to lay hold of him who is utterly desirable.[17]

It is a great joy for me to see this sedum roof. This is a living reality that is symbolic of the heart's journey through life. Just as the roof changes with each season, so too the heart has its seasons of Spring, Summer, Autumn and Winter. Do not be afraid of the changing seasons within your own heart but be attentive   to   them. Allow God to speak through them and reverence the rhythm of death and resurrection both in nature and in your heart.

There is a gradual descent as we draw closer to the entrance. The Portiuncula was built at a much lower level than the surrounding garden. This gives us a sense of entering into the depths of our hearts, and into the depths of the heart of God which Scripture so eloquently describes in the language of love. 'I am going to seduce her and lead her into the desert and speak to her heart.'[18] Let us pause in anticipation as we approach the front door and ponder those beautiful words from the Song of Songs: 'My Beloved put his hand to the hatch, and my heart was thrilled within me.'[19]

THE ENTRANCE

Now that we are inside this dwelling place of God, our Mother Mary is the first to greet us, surrounded as she is by the holy angels. I have always embraced the Mother of God with inexpressible love, because she gave Jesus to us in human flesh. Writing for my brothers and sisters, I

reminded them of the tremendous love of God our Father in giving us his Son, through the Blessed Virgin Mary:

> The most high Father made known from heaven through His holy angel Gabriel this Word of the Father – so worthy, so holy and glorious – in the womb of the holy and glorious Virgin Mary, from whose womb He received the flesh of our humanity and frailty.[20]

With great joy, I entrusted my own spiritual journey to the Virgin Mother of God. I insistently begged her who had conceived and brought to birth the Word full of grace and truth, to become my advocate too.[21] Later I entrusted all my spiritual family to her care and protection. I asked Mary, the Advocate of the Poor, to protect and cherish my family to the end. It greatly consoled and pleased the brothers that Mary became the Advocate of the Order.[22] I even composed my own Praises in her honour. Maybe we could stop for a moment now and pray them together.

> Hail, O Lady,
> Holy Queen,
> Mary, holy Mother of God:
> Who are the virgin made church
> chosen by the most Holy Father in heaven
> whom he consecrated with His most holy beloved Son
> and with the Holy Spirit the Paraclete,
> in whom there was and is
> all the fullness of grace and every good.
> Hail, His Palace!
> Hail, His Tabernacle!
> Hail, His Dwelling!
> Hail, His Robe!
> Hail, His Servant!
> Hail, His Mother! . . .[23]

St Mary of the Angels. How I love that title. I often associate Our Lady with the angels and I often experienced the celestial presence of angels in the Portiuncula. In the *Rule* I wrote for the brothers, chapter 22 is a prayer of thanksgiving to God for the many ways in which his love is revealed to us including the gift of Mary and the angels:

> Because of Your love,
> we humbly beg
> the glorious Mother, the most blessed, ever-virgin Mary,
> Blessed Michael, Gabriel, and Raphael,
> all the choirs of the blessed
> seraphim, cherubim, thrones, dominations,
> principalities, powers, virtues,
> angels, archangels . . . to give You thanks . . .[24]

Yes, I love angels and reminded my brothers and sisters that the angels long to gaze upon the One whom we receive, body, blood, soul and divinity in the Holy Eucharist here on earth. In them, the angels and the saints, God is present, enlightening them to know, inflaming them to love and dwelling in them filling them with happiness.[25] He dwells within you, too, enlightening you to know, inflaming you to love and filling you with happiness. We will return to the angels again as we journey.

THE CHAPEL

The chapel has a cave-like entrance. Caves have fascinated me from my early days. In Assisi and the surrounding areas of remoteness and beauty, I spent long hours in caves and you can still visit them there today. It is not always easy to spend time in soli-tude but I sensed it was the place of personal choice and discovery, so I persevered in search of the hidden treasure. After many long periods of prayer and solitude, I very gradually began to grasp the wonder of the journey inwards and the infinite love with which God draws his children to himself. For me, entering into the cave was also entering into the cave of my heart and what an adventure that is! The fact that you are here now walking the heart's journey with me is a gift of love from God to you. Let us pause for a moment of thanksgiving.

> All-powerful, most holy,
> Almighty and supreme God,
> *Holy* and just *Father,*
> *Lord* King *of heaven and earth*
> we thank You for Yourself
> for through Your holy will
> and through Your only Son
> with the Holy Spirit
> You have created everything . . .

> We thank You
> for as through Your Son You created us,
> so through Your holy love
> *with which You loved us*
> You brought about His birth
> as true God and true man
> by the glorious, ever-virgin, most blessed, holy Mary . . .[26]

With thanksgiving in our hearts, let us enter the chapel together. Notice the shape. This circle is a reminder of the eternity of God without beginning or end. Allow yourself to be enfolded within this circle of Trinitarian love of Father, Son and Holy Spirit. Yes, we are entering into a great mystery. With Christ our brother we are children of the one Father who welcomes us with open arms and open heart. Remain within this all-embracing circle of life and love and allow yourself to be loved. Don't rush this precious moment. Be present with Jesus, our brother.

> O how holy and how loving, gratifying, humbling, peace-giving, sweet, worthy of love, and above all things desirable it is to have such a Brother, our Lord Jesus Christ, Who laid down His life for His sheep and prayed to His Father, saying: *Holy Father save in your name those you have given me.*[27]

He loves us so much! Let us focus on his Real Presence in the Tabernacle.

THE TABERNACLE

The Tabernacle is also circular in shape, emphasizing the centrality of Christ, living and present with us under the form of a tiny piece of bread. Often gaze upon Christ present in the Tabernacle. I know it requires a great act of faith but I used to remind the brothers that just as the Apostles saw the flesh of Jesus and believed he was God,  as they contemplated him with their spiritual eyes, so let us, as we see bread and wine with our bodily eyes, see and firmly believe that they are his most holy body and blood living and true. In this way Jesus is always with us, as he himself says: 'Behold, I am with you until the end of the age.'[28] When I wrote a letter to the entire Order reminding them of the wonder and awe of such a mystery of love, this is what I wrote:

O sublime humility!
O humble sublimity!
The Lord of the universe,
God and the Son of God,
so humbles Himself
that for our salvation
He hides Himself
under an ordinary piece of bread![29]

The colour of the Tabernacle is gold and red. In iconography, gold symbolizes the transcendence of the Godhead and red symbolizes humanity and love, thus revealing the totality of love in the Real Presence of the divine and human Christ. As you gaze at the Tabernacle I repeat to you what I said to the brothers so many years ago:

Look, at the humility of God,
and pour out your hearts before Him![30]

THE SANCTUARY LAMP

The sanctuary lamp, in the shape of a flame, is close to the Tabernacle and highlights the Real Presence of Christ. In sacred Scripture, fiery flames often reveal the presence of God and his all-consuming love for each one of us. In the Old Testament we have only to think of Moses on Mount Horeb, drawn by the burning bush revealing the divine presence as a consuming fire in glory and holiness.[31] The same divine presence, as a pillar of fire, guided the People of Israel through their long and arduous desert experience.[32] In the New Testament Jesus himself said he had come to cast fire upon the earth.[33] This he did through his passion, death and resurrection, sending us his Holy Spirit as flames of divine fire so that we can live through love in his presence.

THE CRUCIFIX

Above the tabernacle is the crucifix. Whenever I look at a crucifix I can hardly keep from weeping. As you know it was from the Cross my beloved Lord spoke so tenderly to me at the beginning of my heart's journey. I realize that from that momentous encounter, this image was deeply impressed in the innermost recesses of my heart and remained with me.[34] Ever since, when I look upon my crucified Lord, my heart melts within me and I can hardly keep from weeping and sighing. The call to love is most eloquently expressed in the love of our crucified Saviour on the Cross. Every time I look at the crucifix I am filled with love and compassion knowing that Jesus embraced our brokenness, frailty and vulnerability by becoming one of us and giving his very life for us. Writing to all my brothers and sisters I appealed to their hearts saying:

> Let *every creature*
> *in heaven, on earth, in the sea* and in the depths,
> give praise, *glory, honour and blessing*
> to Him Who suffered so much.[35]

I also wrote an *Office of the Passion*. Both Clare and myself prayed this Office every day as we entered into the self-giving love of Jesus. Somehow this *Office of the Passion* allowed us into the very heart of the Son. Christ on the Cross reflects the suffering and love that is the raw material of every person's life, and invites a response. In this response our hearts are formed, reformed and transformed in bearing the mystery of our own uniqueness. You may find as I did, in the peace and silence of prayerful solitude, that your unique reflection of God will become clearer and you will see with the eyes of your heart what hope his call holds for you. Be attentive. Be expectant.

At the end of my life I could say to the brothers: I know Christ, poor and crucified.[36] I pray that you too, will enter into the mystery of Christ, poor and crucified for love of you. Sometime during your time in solitude, you may wish to read from St Paul's Letter to the Philippians 2:5–11. Allow those words to sink into your heart and be attentive to the image of Jesus that is revealed in and through these inspired words.

OUR LADY'S STATUE

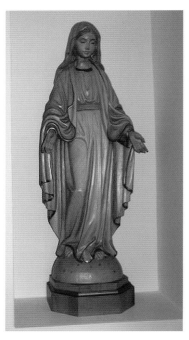

Mary is placed in this chapel to the right of the Tabernacle because Mary was the first Tabernacle for Jesus. When I wrote my Praises in her honour, I too hailed Mary as his Tabernacle.[37] Pope John Paul movingly reminds us of the profound relationship Mary has with the Eucharist: 'With the same maternal concern which she showed at the wedding feast of Cana, Mary seems to say to us: 'Do not waver; trust in the words of my Son. If he was able to change water into wine, he can also turn bread and wine into his body and blood, and through this mystery bestow on believers the living memorial of his Passover, thus becoming the bread of life.' In a certain sense Mary lived her *Eucharistic faith* even before the institution of the Eucharist, by the very fact that *she offered her virginal womb for the Incarnation of God's Word*.[38]

THE STAINED-GLASS WINDOWS

Suffering in one form or another was a constant companion during my life. It was after a particularly difficult night of suffering that my heart was awakened anew by God's grace. With the light of a new day, with the eyes of my heart – for I was almost blind at the time – I too saw everything in a new way and all I could do was sing. I've always loved music and song; it was a vehicle for me to the divine. And so I composed my *Canticle of the Creatures* that you see depicted in symbolic form in these two beautiful windows. I am pleased that my *Canticle* is depicted in stained-glass windows because there is a sense in which

 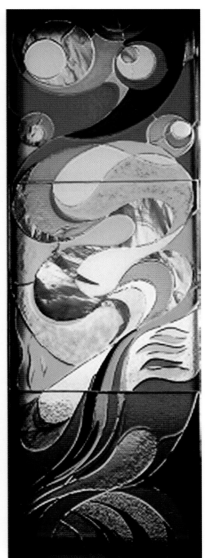

creation itself is a window reflecting the overflowing love and goodness of our God.

Growing up in Assisi, I was very blessed to be surrounded by mountains and valleys, fields and flowers and lakes and streams. I loved the outdoors and my heart and soul seemed to expand as I breathed in the pure air of my native Assisi as I listened to the birds and watched their winged flight in the freedom of the heavenly Father's care of them. You too, in this experience of solitude, will learn to celebrate the great communion we have in Christ with the whole of creation. When I entered into this experience, I called every creature of God, my sister and my brother. Let us pray the *Canticle* together.

> Most High, all-powerful, good Lord,
>   Yours are *the praises, the glory, and the honour*, and all *blessing,*
> To You alone, Most High, do they belong,
>   and no human is worthy to mention Your name.
> Praised be You, my *Lord,* with all *Your creatures,*
>   especially Sir Brother Sun,
>   Who is the day and through whom You give us light.
> And he is beautiful and radiant with great splendour;
>   and bears a likeness of You, Most High One.
> *Praised* be You, my Lord, through Sister *Moon and the stars,*
>   in heaven You formed them clear and precious and beautiful.
>
> Praised be You, my Lord, through Brother Wind,
>   and through the air, cloudy and serene, and every kind of
>   weather,
>   through whom You give sustenance to Your creatures.
> *Praised* be You, my Lord, through Sister *Water,*
>   who is very useful and humble and precious and chaste.
> *Praised* be You, my Lord, through Brother *Fire,*
>   through whom *You light the night,*
>   and he is beautiful and playful and robust and strong.
> *Praised* be You, my Lord, through our Sister Mother *Earth,*
>   who sustains and governs us,
>   and who produces various *fruit* with coloured flowers and
>   *herbs.*
>
> Praised be You, my Lord, through those who give pardon for Your
>   love,
>   and bear infirmity and tribulation.
>   Blessed are those who endure in peace
>   for by You alone Most High, shall they be crowned.
>
> Praised be You, my Lord, through our Sister Bodily Death,
>   from whom no one living can escape.

Woe to those who die in mortal sin.
Blessed are those whom death will find in Your most holy will,
for the second death shall do them no harm.

Praise and *bless* my Lord and give Him thanks
and serve Him with great humility.[39]

Maybe you also feel inspired to compose and pray your own Canticle of Praise for the gift and beauty of creation.

THE SEVEN SMALL WINDOWS

The number of smaller windows in this chapel is also symbolic. In Scripture and indeed in every culture the number seven is significant. In the Book of Revelation we are told that there are seven angels, like burning lamps, in front of the throne of God.[40] They are also called angels of The Presence. In the Book of Genesis we are told that God rested on the seventh day representing the complete and perfect work of creation.[41] In St Luke's Gospel the number seven is used in connection with the perfection of forgiveness and love.[42] In keeping with the spirituality of the Portiuncula, especially our focus on angels and peace and reconciliation, we highlight the perfection of love to which we are all called in our life with God and with each other.

THE FOUR ANGELS

We are back again to angels and to the symbolism of numbers. Four in Scripture always refers to the universe or this created world. There are four niches in the chapel within which is a picture of an angel. The Book of Revelation refers to the angels who stand around the throne of God and who day and night never stop singing: Holy, Holy, Holy, is the Lord God Almighty, Who was, and is and is to come.[43] These four angels are also associated with their mission to the four corners of the earth.

What a world of mystery surrounds us in our love relation-ship with God. In his great tenderness, God our loving Father gifts us with heavenly spirits to comfort, console, help and guide us as we journey to him. Before we leave the chapel, let us pause for a moment and with Our Lady and the angels, let us adore, praise and thank the Good God in the prayer I loved to pray daily and indeed many times during the day.

All-powerful, most holy,
most high, and supreme God:
all good,
supreme good,
totally good,
You Who *alone are good*,
may we give You
all praise, all *glory*,
all thanks, all *honour*:
all blessing
and all good.
So be it!
So be it!
Amen.[44]

THE CONTEMPLATION SPACE

There was a time in my life when I could not decide whether God was calling me to a life of preaching or a life of contemplation. I resolved the question by asking the advice of Clare and Sylvester, two companions whose discernment I trusted. Following their counsel, I gave my life to both active ministry and prolonged prayer in a rhythm that helped me to follow in the footsteps of Jesus Christ my Lord. Jesus spent himself in active ministry and also in prolonged prayer. I felt very happy with that rhythm in my life too. In fact I even wrote a little *Rule for Hermitages*[45] for those who wish to spend some time solitude.

In Scripture there is a story about two sisters called Martha and Mary. Let me remind you of it because in my little *Rule for Hermitages* I mention Martha and Mary, assuming that most people are familiar with the story and its implications. St Luke tells the story:

In the course of their journey he came to a village, and a woman named Martha welcomed him into her house. She had a sister called Mary, who sat down at the Lord's feet and listened to him speaking. Now Martha, who was distracted with all the serving, came to him and said, 'Lord, do you not care that my sister is leaving me to do the serving all by myself? Please tell her to help me.' But the Lord answered, 'Martha, Martha,' he said, 'you worry and fret about so many things, and yet few are needed, indeed only one. It is Mary who has chosen the better part, and it is not to be taken from her.'[46]

Here we are in the realm of the tension that often exists between our work and our prayer. As I have already mentioned, I too struggled with this tension within my own heart until I faced it, prayed about it and sought discernment from my prayerful friends. For me, it was not an *either/or* choice. It was rather a call and response to integrate both Martha and Mary within my own heart. Normally we speak about good, better and best. I now realize that for me the best choice involved deep solitary prayer and intense loving activity. This rhythm I built into my daily life in imitation of Jesus my Lord.

The Portiuncula captures that rhythm of the loving service of Martha and the contemplative prayer of Mary not only in the lived experience here, but also within the very building itself. The chapel opens into a beautiful and spacious prayer area specifically dedicated to the Blessed Trinity: the Father, the Son and the Holy Spirit. To the right of the Contemplation Space are the hermitages – the Mary side where you have a personal, sacred space to sit at the feet of the Lord and listen to his words. To the left is the Martha side where you meet and minister to each other in word and deed as you share the journey. Significantly, it is the prayer space between the two that provides the link and rhythm that is fundamental to my vision of living in this world. Here in this sacred space I hope and pray that you will receive grace and insight into your life and experiences that will empower you to live your life to the full in both rest and activity. Jesus said: 'I have come that you may life and have it to the full.'[47]

As you enter into the centre of the Contemplation Space, you are drawn symbolically into the centre of the life of the Trinity. Let us sit for a moment on the specially designed seat that gives us a sense of enclosure within the heart of the Trinity. I was always insistent that the time of solitude should be protected as far as possible from all noise and distraction. Gentle lighting enfolds you from above and below. The two circular skylights are a reminder that Christ is both the first and the last. 'I am the Alpha and the Omega, says the Lord God, who is, who was, and who is to come, the Almighty.'[48]

The three stained-glass panels within the seating represent the Trinity, and the symbolic palm and olive branches, speak of suffering-love and peace. Here you will learn of the unfathomable love of God for you and the gift of his peace with which he desires to fill your heart. The Father, the Son and the Holy Spirit welcome you and desire to reveal to you the love that exists for you in the heart of God from all eternity.

THE FOUNTAIN

Within the circle of the Trinity, let us be still before this fountain and ponder the constant and never-ending cycle of overflowing water emerging and returning to its source. My dear brother, St Bonaventure, wrote very eloquently about the symbolism of the fountain. He described the Father as the fountain-fullness of overflowing goodness and love. Yes, our tender, most holy and loving Father shares his very life with us by giving us Jesus, his son and our brother, with the Holy Spirit, the gift we must desire above all else.

Gaze upon the water that is overflowing. The goodness and love which it symbolizes is also overflowing, life giving, constant, gentle and in abundance for you. When you pray before this fountain allow the life and love of the Father to fill your heart. You may also wish to spend some time pondering those beautiful words of Jesus in St John's Gospel when he spent time at the well with the Samaritan woman and also when he invited each of us to quench our thirst at the fount of his love.[49]

Know too, that the water that flows here is a symbol of the universality of the Gospel in its life-giving and healing mission to all people. Today, in an age where travel is so easy, there is a sense in which the world is a global village. I always liked to see myself as a pilgrim in this world and so I am pleased that the water that flows here has come from many places of pilgrimage in many different parts of the world. There is water that was blessed at the Easter Vigil in the local Parish of Christ the King, Alfreton, Derbyshire and was used to baptize new brothers and sisters who were received into full communion on that wonderful Feast. It is good to ponder the gift of Baptism and to revisit that momentous occasion. There is water from the Holy Land, from both the River Jordan and the Dead Sea. As this building is dedicated to Our Blessed Lady, there is water here from many of her healing shrines: Lourdes in France; Fatima in Portugal; Walsingham in England; Knock in Ireland, Carfin in Scotland; Medugjorge in Yugoslavia; Czestochowa in Poland and Ngome in South Africa. There is also water from shrines associated with saints who have journeyed into their own hearts as pilgrims and penitents: St Patrick in Lough Derg and St Columba in Donegal, both in Ireland. It is encouraging to know that you are in the company of so many who have journeyed before you and now wish to befriend you on your own journey. Therefore, take heart and be open to the healing water welling up within you.

STONES AGAIN

Around the fountain are a great number of white stones. These too have a symbolic value. In the Book of Revelation we read the beautiful words: 'To those who prove victorious I will give some hidden manna and a white stone, with a new name written on it, known only to the person who receives it.'[50]

It is an awesome thought that you and I have existed in God from all eternity – even before we came to birth on this earth. Not only does his love desire us, he even has a dream and a plan for our lives as we reflect the image of his only-begotten Son, Jesus. This is why I always impressed on my brothers and companions that just as I tried to fulfil God's plan for my life, each of them had to discover their call and live it to the full. You may already be familiar with my exact words:

I have done what is mine; may Christ teach you yours.[51]

Let us gaze at these white stones as we give thanks together for the wonder of our creation and for the love that has held us in the heart of God from all eternity. Of course that love was given and received most fully in Jesus, our brother, so let us turn to the crucifix before which I prayed so fervently to know the will of God for me.

THE SAN DAMIANO CROSS

It moves me very deeply to see a replica of the San Damiano cross here. The original is in my beloved Assisi. What memories I desire to share with you as we gaze upon our Lord and Saviour, Jesus Christ in this icon. I will briefly relate what happened to me on that momentous day when I stopped by to pray for direction in my life. I so much desired to get in touch with my restless heart and discover what the Father dreamed for me from all eternity.

When I went into the little chapel, it was broken down and very dilapidated but the large cross drew me to itself and I fell to my knees. I don't know how long I was there. All I know is that I poured out my heart to the One who holds our lives and destiny in his hands and heart and I prayed. Some words I do remember and you may wish to pray them with me now, especially if you are seeking to discover God's dream for you and what it is he is asking of you at this particular time in your life. I know now that all he desires for us is our good, our happiness and our joy. Let us pray together:

> Most High,
> glorious God
> enlighten the darkness of my heart
> and give me
> true faith,
> certain hope
> and perfect charity,
> sense and knowledge
> Lord,
> that I may carry out
> Your holy and true command.[52]

And my prayer was answered. I heard words from Christ on the Cross and I was moved to my very depths. I was asked to repair the church of Christ that was falling into ruin. What a mission! What an invitation! What a privilege! What a responsibility! I, Francis Bernardone, called by name from on high, was entrusted with the repair of the church of Christ! Overjoyed, I could hardly wait to get started. I thought I understood perfectly what the Lord was asking of me. Later I would learn that the physical repair of this little church was only a first step on the journey.

Yes, Jesus with arms outstretched welcomes you too. Look into his eyes and experience his love for you as I did at the beginning of my heart's journey. In the silence, he will speak to your heart. Here in the presence of Mary his mother, and with the angels and the saints surrounding him, you will be drawn into his embrace, as you desire in love to know him more intimately and do his holy will. You will return to this cross again and again. I did. Clare did. My brothers and sisters still do. In your repeated encounters you will also meet Mary, the saints and the angels who also speak their message from within this holy gathering.

It was Clare who treasured this crucifix in a special way. It was a bond between us even after my death. She knew what it meant for me. She knew how my journey changed direction from the moment I heard those words from the Crucified. Every day Clare gazed on that crucifix and as her journey continued, love deepened and transformed her. We know this because she tells us how it came about as she gazed upon this cross. It became for her a mirror in which she saw clearly the passionate love of her crucified Spouse and the call to imitate the virtues reflected there. Her words to Agnes of Prague are also an invitation and a challenge to you as you now gaze on this San Damiano cross.

> Gaze upon that mirror each day, O Queen and Spouse of Jesus Christ, and continually study your face within it ... [53]
> And *transform* your entire being *into the image*
> of the Godhead Itself through contemplation.[54]

THE HOLY SPIRIT

I loved to tell the brothers that the Holy Spirit was the real Minister General of our Order. I now say to you what I said so many years ago:

Pay attention to what you must desire above all else: to have the Spirit of the Lord and Its holy activity.[55]

In Scripture, the Holy Spirit is symbolized as a dove. Here too we have expressed the presence of the Holy Spirit under this form. The medium is glass because of the elusive and transparent characteristics we associate with the Holy Spirit. The gold within the glass speaks of transcendence and the reality of the mystery in which we are immersed. Following the scriptural symbolism of Pentecost, we have the flames of fire descending upon us to inflame our hearts with love of God and one another.

Sometime you may wish to reflect on the Admonitions I wrote for my brothers and sisters.[56] There I tried to set out very clearly the many ways in which we can recognize the holy operations of the Spirit of God as opposed to the spirit of selfishness and sin. You will experience this new life within yourself as you turn your heart to the Lord. His Holy Spirit will rest upon you and you will become his dwelling place. This is an awesome reality. You might like to meditate on these promises during your time in solitude. Immersed as we are in the life and love of the Trinity, it is the Holy Spirit who will reveal to you and effect within you the filial relationship you have with the Father and the spousal relationship you have with Jesus. The Holy Spirit is the Spirit of Love. Let us pray together:

Almighty, eternal, just and merciful God,
give us miserable ones
the grace to do for You alone
what we know you want us to do
and always to desire what pleases You.
Inwardly cleansed,
interiorly enlightened,
and inflamed by the fire of the Holy Spirit,
may we be able to follow
in the footprints of Your beloved Son,
our Lord Jesus Christ,
and, by Your grace alone,
may we make our way to You,
Most High,
Who live and rule
in perfect Trinity and simple Unity,
and are glorified
God almighty,
forever and ever.
Amen.[57]

THE TAU

At the end of the Contemplation Space you will see a statue of myself holding the Tau Cross.[58] I must say a word about the Tau Cross because it meant so much to me during my conversion journey. I used to draw it at the end of my letters and I also used to draw it above the doors and walls of the cells of the brothers. Really it became part of my personal signature and coat of arms, so I must speak of it now.

There was a Council in Rome in 1215. It was the Fourth Lateran Council and Pope Innocent III chose the Passover and the Tau as the theme of his preaching. My already very enthusiastic desire to live according to the Holy Gospel was set aflame anew and my heart was deeply touched by what I heard. I wanted to accept the challenge of the Council and preach conversion of heart to all my sisters and brothers. I was particularly struck by the way in which His Holiness, Pope Innocent III, developed the theme of the Passover with special reference to the symbol of the Tau. His words were written indelibly into my heart, especially when I heard him say: 'Mercy will be granted to those who bear the Tau, a mark of a life of penance and renewal in Christ.' I was already familiar with those words of the prophet Ezekiel who was commanded to mark with the Tau all who weep because of the sin of the world.[59] Fired with a new zeal for preaching, in the words of the Pope, I felt a personal mandate to be a champion of the Tau and of the cross. Therefore, to be sealed with this sign is to experience the joy of a heart turned in love to the Lord and to know that we desire to glory in nothing except the Cross of our Lord Jesus Christ.

For me the Tau has another very significant aspect that is the fruit of a converted heart. It is the call to compassion. For me, the Tau has always been associated with showing mercy especially to my brother lepers. Perhaps one of the greatest crosses for any person in any period of history is to feel rejected and marginalized by your brothers and sisters in society. In my day, it was the leper who was the outcast and I was deeply inspired and impressed by the Hospital Brothers of Saint Antony the Hermit who cared for lepers. In fact they allowed me the privilege of caring for my brother lepers in their hospitals and I was fascinated by the large Tau symbol on their religious habits. I learned that this symbol was directly related to their care for lepers. The Tau, representing the Cross of Christ was a sign of health, wholeness and salvation through Jesus Christ, crucified and risen.

I felt very drawn to the richness and depth hidden in this simple sign, so that when Pope Innocent III chose it as the theme of his preaching at the Lateran Council, I was on fire within not only to proclaim the message of conversion of heart but also to serve my brother lepers with renewed zeal, remembering how the prophet Isaiah had described the Suffering Servant, who, like

my brother lepers was despised and rejected. Jesus, the Suffering Servant of God, knew what it was like when people looked away because physical suffering disfigured his outward appearance and hid the beauty that was within. That is why I told my brothers to rejoice when they live among people considered of little value and looked down upon, among the poor and the powerless, the sick and the lepers and the beggars by the wayside.[60] There is a great mystery here and I would encourage you to ponder and pray more deeply about this and ask Jesus to open the eyes and ears of your heart.

May I now trace the sign of the Tau on your forehead that you too may experience mercy and renewal in the joy of salvation through the Cross of our Lord Jesus Christ? You may even feel drawn to wearing the Tau as a constant reminder of the love within which you are held and the Cross through which the whole world has been redeemed. It is indeed a symbol of great hope, encouragement and daily conversion to love. It may also remind you that I walk with you on your faith journey.

THE HERMITAGES

You will notice that the building falls naturally into two sides with the Contemplation Space linking both. This is a simple way of expressing the Gospel truth that in our everyday lives we have a rhythm of action and contemplation and our life of love in the embrace of the Trinity encompasses both. Yes, love is the key. Therefore, in Gospel terms we are both Martha and Mary as we journey in love through our earthly life. That Gospel passage about Martha and Mary has been the cause of much controversy since the time of Jesus to our present day.

As I have already mentioned, I know the experience and tension of feeling attracted wholeheartedly to either Martha or Mary. With prayerful discernment, experience and time I have learned that life is not really an either/or choice but it is possible to integrate both prayer and action when love is the motivating energy informing both. It is the way that Jesus the Son of God chose for himself while on earth. He has identified with us in our blessedness and our brokenness. Now that you have come apart to rest for a while, you too will become more vulnerable as you accept your blessedness and your brokenness. I will humbly and gratefully tell you how the Good Lord worked in my life during my periods of solitude. It was not always easy but solitude was and is one way to pierce through the illusions and meet the Truth.

God bestowed upon me, your little, poor brother, Francis, many singular graces and blessings. He will do great things for you too if you open your heart to his love. Therefore, I say to you what I said to my brothers and sisters when I was with them: Hold back nothing of yourselves for yourselves, that he Who gives Himself totally to you may receive you totally![61] Let us begin with Greccio.

GRECCIO HERMITAGE[62]

Let me take you back to Christmas 1223. It was in the Rieti Valley in a hermitage reminiscent of the cave where our dear Saviour was born, that my dear friends and I joined in the celebration of Midnight Mass. Eager to recall and relive that awesome moment of our God taking our flesh and becoming one of us, I desired to have a manger filled with hay and an ox and an ass standing by — just like that first Christmas midnight. And so it was. Beneath the altar the first crib was made and with great joy the Mass began. But I was not prepared for what happened next. It seemed to me that the child in the crib was pulsing with life and love. I took him in my arms and I understood in a new way the meaning of Emmanuel: God-with-us. Oh! I cannot put into words the depth of that experience, but its meaning and reality for every person and for all time is something I desire every person to know. It pleases me that the custom of making Christmas 'come alive' in the making of Christmas cribs, has spread far and wide and brings such joy to young and old alike. May it always be an experience of God being born anew in each person's heart. Now you will understand why Greccio is often called 'The Franciscan Bethlehem'.

As you enter Greccio hermitage, praise, adore and thank our loving Father-God for giving us his only Son to walk this earth with us, as one of us in flesh and blood. What a tremendous mystery that God should become a human being! I still want to go down on my knees and weep with love and gratitude for the gift of God in human flesh. It seems to me that God wishes us to approach him with very great love and without fear. After all, no one is afraid of a child! A child invites us to an embrace, a kiss, a tender caring and nurturing. Is this how you experience God? If not, are you open to this experience now?

Greccio also celebrates God's continuing presence with us: body, blood, soul and divinity in the Holy Eucharist. Only God could think of such a gift for staying with us until the end of time. I have already spoken to you about this wonderful gift when we visited the chapel, but now I wish to link it with Greccio because of his enduring and real presence under the form of humble bread. Again, it is the Greccio experience of giving birth and nurturing that I see so clearly when I think of the Eucharist. Yes, you are invited to give birth to God in the world around you and to nurture goodness in your brothers and sisters by the love and joy you radiate. But you are also invited to allow yourself to be 'mothered' and ministered to by God, by Mary, by the angels and saints and by your brothers and sisters with whom you are sharing this experience.

I am very sensitive to all the gifts that God has given me as a human person. The gifts of sight, hearing, smell, taste and touch have always been the channels to draw me closer to God. Therefore, become aware of these gifts during your time in solitude. Notice the colour of your hermitage. It is blue because in iconography blue symbolizes the heavens and divinity. It also symbolizes humility. Just being enfolded in a blue hermitage will remind you of the mystery of divine life hidden within the humanity of a little child and in the humble bread of the Eucharist. This divine life is also hidden within you! It is good to thank God for the wonder of your being. You are God's gift and a unique expression of his life and love in this world. I used to tell the brothers and I repeat it to you now:

> Consider, O human being, in what great excellence the Lord God has placed you, for He created and formed you to the image of His beloved Son according to the body and to His likeness according to the Spirit.[63]

POGGIO BUSTONI HERMITAGE[64]

If you are like me you will associate certain places with certain experiences and memories. All my hermitages in Assisi were places of special graces for me and Poggio Bustoni was no exception. I don't know how long you have lived and what your experiences in life have been, but you may be able to identify with some of the feelings and anxieties I had during my stay at Poggio Bustoni. I pray you will also receive the special graces associated with this place.

When I went to Poggio Bustoni, I was full of hopes and fears, doubts and dreams, anxieties and worries, not only about my past but also about the future. About my past, I was fearful because of the way I had lived my life before my conversion to the Lord. It is amazing the way intimacy with the Lord brings new awareness and insight. Anyway, in that cave in Poggio Bustoni, I was filled with a certain anxiety about the sins of my youth and the ways I had squandered the gifts of grace. Then I remembered the brothers whom I had left outside the cave and I was filled with another kind of anxiety about their future – our future. It was in the midst of this turmoil that I cried out: Lord, be merciful to me a sinner. I don't know how many times I repeated this prayer but gradually I was so aware of a tremendous and indescribable joy welling up within me.

In that moment all my darkness and bitterness and anxiety faded away. I experienced the tender mercy of God and the assurance that my past could be left to his mercy and my future to his providence. What a release I experienced in that moment of overwhelming grace. I felt enfolded in love and mercy. My heart was full of joy and confidence. My soul was filled with the light of God's grace and my spirit soared to new heights in the embrace of his tender mercy and love. I returned to the brothers that day renewed, rejoicing and in a sense, transformed. They noticed it too![65]

In this hermitage, I knew the meaning of goodness: the goodness of God, the goodness of myself, the goodness of every other brother and sister, the goodness of all creation. Even today, the people in Poggio Bustoni repeat my greeting: 'Good morning, good people'. Yes, the hermitage of Poggio

Bustoni will forever be associated with goodness, peace, reconciliation, mercy and mission. From here I wanted to proclaim to the whole world the tender mercy of God and invite everyone to come to him to receive pardon and peace. I pray that this may be your experience too.

Let *every creature*
in heaven, on earth, in the sea and in the depths,
give praise, *glory, honour and blessing*
To Him Who suffered so much,
Who has given and will give in the future every good,
for He is our power and our strength,
Who *alone is good*,
Who alone is almighty,
Who alone is omnipotent, wonderful, glorious
and Who alone is holy,
worthy of praise and blessing
through endless ages.
Amen.[66]

The colour of the Poggio Bustoni hermitage is a pale shade of purple. In iconography the colour purple symbolizes power, and in the Liturgy purple is associated with repentance. I hope that when you are aware of the colour of your surroundings here, you will be reminded of the power of God's tender love and mercy and your own desire to repent and have your sins forgiven. Every day is a new day to turn your heart to the Lord. Allow it to happen. Be cleansed. Be healed of your burdens. Be touched by God. He is waiting for you.

THE CARCERI HERMITAGE[67]

I loved mountains and woods and often went to the beautiful and remote hermitage, the Carceri. Some people translate 'carceri' literally and think of a type of prison. But that is not how I see it at all. Carceri for me is that special place of seclusion where I learned the secret of solitude. In that place of silence and seclusion, I discovered something very wonderful. I discovered that our tender, loving and good God desired to liberate me from whatever imprisoned me from within, revealing my true identity in him. In these intimate moments there were times when as a beloved child, from the depths of my heart I entreated my God as Father. At other times I play-fully conversed with my God who is spouse to me. And at other times, I spoke with my God, heart to heart, as a friend.[68] You too will find yourself in heart to heart intimacy with God who desires so much to reveal your true identity in him. But to really listen requires time and space and silence.

The colour of the Carceri is yellow. In iconography, yellow symbolizes Truth. Here in the Carceri, the Truth will set you free from all that imprisons you. The colour yellow also represents the light, happiness and joy associated with being set free from the darkness of sin and selfishness to live your new life in Christ: the experience of being a child, a friend and a spouse within the life and love of the Blessed Trinity.

FONTE COLUMBO HERMITAGE[69]

I have so many memories associated with this hermitage. It was a great thrill for me to discover several doves drinking from a small spring of beautiful clear water. Therefore, it seemed natural for me to name this hermitage, Fonte Columbo meaning Fountain of the Doves. It was here that I wrote a *Rule of Life* based on the words of the holy Gospel. I simply wanted to walk in the footsteps of my beloved Lord and so I turned to the Gospel for direction and guidance. I think this is why Fonte Columbo is often referred to as 'The Franciscan Sinai'. Imagine comparing me to Moses! Well, I suppose just as Moses gave the Israelites the Ten Commandments as a way of life, so I too gave the Gospel as a way of life. Those who came after me preserved this memory for all time by writing the following words for all pilgrims to this hermitage:

> May the Holy Spirit who conducted Francis to this Sinai, grant you, the pilgrim, the grace to renew yourself.

I pray that the Holy Spirit will renew you during your stay here in Fonte Columbo. This will happen especially as you open your heart to the Word of God. I wish everyone would realize the gift of the Living Word of God. Perhaps each day you may find time to ponder the Word of God in your heart and you will slowly realize that you too are a 'word in the Word'. This awareness of your uniqueness as a word of God made flesh in this world with your own particular vocation and mission will fill your heart with gratitude, praise and joy in the Lord. Perhaps we can pause here and pray that the will of God may be fully realized in your life and that you will discover your true identity in him.

> *Your will be done on earth as in heaven:*
> That we may love You
> with our whole heart by always thinking of You,
> with our whole soul by always desiring You,
> with our whole mind by always directing all our intentions to You,
> and by seeking Your glory in everything,
> with all our whole strength by exerting
> all our energies and affections of body and soul
> in the service of Your love and of nothing else;
> and we may love our neighbour as ourselves
> by drawing them all to Your love with our whole strength,
> by rejoicing in the good of others as in our own,
> by suffering with others at their misfortunes
> and by giving offence to no one.[70]

Fonte Columbo also reminds me of the painful eye disease I had. The brothers were very kind to me and wished to alleviate my pain by asking the doctor to visit my hermitage and cauterize my eyes. I was fearful of the remedy but I remember praying to Brother Fire in these words:

My Brother Fire, noble and useful among all the creatures the Most High created, be courtly to me in this hour. For a long time I have loved you and I still love you for the love of that Lord who created you. I pray our Creator who made you, to temper your heat now, so that I may bear it.[71]

When I had finished my prayer, I made the Sign of the Cross and Brother Fire did not hurt me at all. I was deeply grateful to God for such a miracle and I always associate Fonte Columbo with the way in which suffering may be embraced in the heart's journey towards healing. Although I was almost physically blind, my spiritual sight became ever clearer as I turned to the Word of God. Jesus promised: 'The words I have spoken to you are spirit and they are life.'[72] Yes, I have many memories of Fonte Columbo and the many miracles the Lord worked there.

The colour of the Fonte Columbo hermitage is green. In iconography green is symbolic of life, growth and hope. May your heart be strengthened in hope as you journey towards healing, wholeness and integration. Open yourself to the Word of God, and experience the spring of living water welling up within you as the fire of love inflames your heart to embrace your vocation and mission in life. Do not be afraid. Let us pray together:

Holy be Your Name:
May knowledge of You become clearer in us
that we may know
the breadth of Your blessings,
the length of Your promises,
the height of Your majesty,
the depth of Your judgments.[73]

LA VERNA HERMITAGE[74]

The holy mountain! 'The Franciscan Calvary'. How I loved La Verna! Already I am filled with deep emotion just telling you about it – though I can never tell all. It was generous Count Orlando who gave me this mountain for prayer and penance. My words seemed to reach deep into his heart and he understood the need for solitude, silence and seclusion in the rugged beauty of the mountains. In fact I was so surprised by this offer of a mountain for prayer that the words of the Count are embedded in my heart. He said: 'Brother Francis, I have a mountain in Tuscany, which is very solitary and wild and perfectly suited for someone who wants to do penance in a remote place or who seeks to live a solitary life. It is called Mount La Verna. If that mountain should please you and your companions, I would gladly give it to you for the salvation of my soul'.[75] He would gladly give it! I have always loved spontaneous generosity. In fact I often got into trouble for this very thing both at home and in the fraternity. There is great joy in giving. I never ceased to be amazed at the way in which our gracious God, in his divine providence, lavishes his gifts upon us through each other. Count Orlando provided for our spiritual and physical needs many times and for this I gave constant praise and thanks to God.

La Verna is a place of very great and austere beauty. It was revealed to me that the massive rocks had been split at the time of our dear Lord's Passion. When I saw these rocks, I experienced an interior conviction that the Passion of Jesus would once again be renewed on this holy mountain. And you know the rest of the story. It has been told and retold many times. Nevertheless, I know you wish me to talk to you about it – in so far as I can.

It was two years before my death. The year was 1224 and it was September, the feast of The Exaltation of the Holy Cross. I had been fasting and praying on this holy mountain and the crucified Christ seemed to be the focus of my prayer. Such love and such suffering! I so much wanted to understand, and I remember saying: Who are you, my dearest God? And what am I, your vilest little worm and useless little servant? Perhaps it was the immensity of the mountain that made me feel so little and insignificant in the awesome and mighty presence of God. To help me find an answer I turned as always to the Word of God in the holy Gospel. Three times Brother Leo and myself opened the Book at the Passion of Christ. In that moment I had an intense desire to be one with my Lord and I prayed a very daring prayer:

> My Lord Jesus Christ, I pray You to grant me two graces before I die. The first is that during my life I may feel in my soul and in my body, as much as possible, that pain that You, dear Jesus, sustained in the hour of Your most bitter passion. The second is that I may feel in my heart, as much as possible, that great love with which You, O Son of God, were inflamed in willingly enduring such suffering for us sinners.[76]

RECEIVING THE STIGMATA

I am not really sure what happened next or how much time elapsed between the prayer and the answer to the prayer. But I could never have imagined how my prayer would be answered. There appeared to me a seraph with six wings gleaming like fire descending from heaven. The seraph appeared as crucified and I knew it was Christ, crucified and risen. I cannot tell you the joy and the sorrow that filled my soul in that encounter. The tenderness of his gaze melted my heart. Compassionate love overwhelmed me and I entered so deeply into the intimate life and love of God that I simply cannot clothe the experience with human words. All I know is that it happened and when the vision ended my soul was on fire with love. It was then I realized just how complete the identification with Christ crucified was. In my body I had received the precious wounds of Christ. My hands, feet and side were pierced with the marks of crucified love. Let us pause for a few moments now because even to recall this experience deeply moves me.

La Verna will always be a place associated with the mystery of suffering and love. For me, it was the culmination, the consolation and the verification of my heart's quest par excellence. What more could the Lord do for me during my earthly journey? He had set his seal on my dream and my destiny and this has meaning for you, my friend, as the Lord leads you to discover your La Verna.

Only few people bear exteriorly the marks of our dear Saviour's wounds but are not all people wounded interiorly by suffering and love? Perhaps this hermitage will help you to revisit all those areas of your life that have been marked by suffering and love. The two are inseparable, and they are part of every human life. But La Verna taught me as it will teach you that God shares our humanity and within this mystery, everything you suffer has meaning and value when love is alive and at work in your heart. Enter the mystery and celebrate God with us in suffering and in love. Let us praise him together in the words that flowed from my heart after that momentous experience:

You are holy Lord God *Who does* wonderful things.

You are strong. *You are great.* You are the most high.
     You are the almighty king. You *holy Father.*
King of heaven and earth.

You are three and one, the Lord God of gods;
     You are good, all good, the highest good,
     Lord God *living and true.*

You are love, charity; You are wisdom, You are humility,
You are patience, You are beauty, You are meekness,
You are security, You are rest,
You are gladness and joy, You are our hope, You are justice,
You are moderation, You are all our riches to sufficiency.

You are beauty, You are meekness,
     You are the protector, You are our custodian and defender,
     You are strength, You are refreshment. You are our hope,
     You are our faith, You are our charity,
     You are all our sweetness, You are our eternal life:
     Great and wonderful Lord, Almighty God, Merciful
Saviour.[77]

BLESSING FOR BROTHER LEO

In La Verna hermitage God will give you the gift of inner peace as he promised. Even amid suffering, turmoil and temptation, the peace of Christ dwells in the heart that is turned to him in love. It was on La Verna that Brother Leo experienced severe temptation but it was also on La Verna that he received peace. I remember writing a little message of consolation for him in the form of a blessing, and I impart this same blessing  to you because you too may be troubled by severe temptation during your solitude experience:

> The Lord bless you and keep you
> May he show his face to you and be merciful to you.
> May he turn his regard towards you and give you peace.
> May the Lord bless you.

Before I left La Verna I entrusted all my brothers to Mary, Mother of the Eternal Word. If you will permit me now, I would also like to entrust you to Mary, Mother of the Eternal Word, knowing that she will form you as a word in The Word. Yes, you are a unique expression of the Word made Flesh, and with God's grace you will continue to become the person God has dreamed of from all eternity. This is the message of La Verna: be transformed into his image, into his likeness, not necessarily by physical martyrdom but by total loving.

> *With our whole heart,*
> *our whole soul,*
> *our whole mind,*
> *with our whole strength and fortitude,*
> *with our whole understanding,*
> with all our powers,
> with every effort,
> every affection,

every feeling,
every desire and wish
Let us all love *the Lord God*
Who has given and gives each one of us
our whole body, our whole soul, and our whole life,
Who has created, redeemed and will save us by His mercy alone,
Who did and does everything good for us ...[78]

Such loving will naturally impel you towards compassionate love for all your brothers and sisters in Christ. When I left La Verna with such an awareness of the suffering Christ in the world, I ardently desired to minister once again to my brother lepers. You too, will return from here, renewed and refreshed as you continue the rhythm of contemplation and compassion in your day-to-day living.

The colour of La Verna hermitage is terracotta. The meaning of the word terracotta is baked earth, a reminder of the fire that burns within your heart. This earthen-red colour is symbolic of the passion of suffering love that lies within your earthliness, burning, transforming, remaking and renewing you in the image and likeness of God who is your Father, your brother and your spouse. Your transformation from within will affect every aspect of your living and relationships. As you honour the rhythm of withdrawing and engaging, prayer and service become one in love.

This rhythm, typified in the story of Martha and Mary, is also apparent in this Portiuncula building. Having spent some time with the 'Mary' side of the building, let us now turn to the 'Martha' side. On this left side of the building we have the kitchen, the dining room, the companion room and the reception office.

SOLITUDE IN FRATERNITY

In my little *Rule for Hermitages*, it seemed good to me to encourage the fraternal aspect in solitude. I desire that each brother and sister has a sacred space but  always remember that you journey together. Therefore, I specifically mentioned that there is a time when you may be free from silence during which time you nurture and nourish each other on the journey. One way of doing this is the beautiful occasion of sharing a meal together to celebrate the gift of friendship and love as we journey to God. Always begin the meal recognizing the goodness of God in the fruits of the earth and the work of human hands and at the same time we pray that all our brothers and sisters may enjoy the necessities of life.

THE KITCHEN

I have already referred to the Martha/Mary rhythm involving both prayer and service. The kitchen gives the opportunity to serve one's brothers and sisters in solitude by providing for their practical, daily needs. In my little *Rule* for those who wish to spend some time in hermitages, I advised taking turns for a time to minister to each other according to mutual decision. This is all part of the shared experience of Franciscan solitude.

BETHANY DINING ROOM

Reflection on the homely scene of Jesus in the house of Martha and Mary in Bethany creates the atmosphere for our shared meal. Just as Jesus sat at table in Bethany, he is here too. Be aware of his presence in your midst because he said he would be present where two or three gather in his name. In your time of solitude, you may wish to meet with your brothers and sisters for the main meal of the day. Though I strongly recommend that you do so, I always respect the holy operation of the Spirit of God in each person. Therefore, if the Holy Spirit suggests that you do not break your silence on a particular day by speaking with others, be faithful and honour the way the Holy Spirit leads you.

NAZARETH COMPANION ROOM

When you enter the experience of Franciscan solitude, you travel in the company of your brothers and sisters. I always encouraged a small number to support one another during the hermitage experience. This Nazareth companion room is a sacred space where you may wish to converse with the person designated as your spiritual companion on the journey. When you do so, it will be with the blessing of the Lord God and in the stance of Mary of Nazareth: attentive, receptive and responsive to the Word of God, bringing it to birth in your life and bearing fruit for the good of the whole human family. I say to you what I said to Brother Leo: If you need and want to come to me for the sake of your soul or for some consolation, come.

ST JOSEPH RECEPTION OFFICE

Finally we have come to St Joseph. This room is near to the entrance where St Joseph is entrusted with the protection of the Portiuncula and all who spend time here. As protector of the Holy Family while on earth, St Joseph will continue his role as protector of our household and a model for our response to both prayer and action. His 'eloquent silence' is of special significance in this solitude experience. I have always had a wonderful relationship with popes. Now I would like to quote a few words from Pope John Paul II in his Apostolic Exhortation on St Joseph:

> In the course of that pilgrimage of faith, which was his life, Joseph, like Mary, remained faithful to God's call until the end. While Mary's life was the bringing to fullness of that fiat first spoken at the Annunciation, at the moment of Joseph's own 'annunciation' he said nothing; instead he simply 'did as the angel of the Lord commanded him' (Mt. 1:24). And this first 'doing' became the beginning of 'Joseph's way.' The Gospels do not record any word ever spoken by Joseph along that way. But the silence of Joseph has its own special eloquence, for thanks to that silence we can understand the truth of the Gospel's judgment that he was 'a just man'. (Mt. 1:19)[79]

THE ICON OF FRANCIS AND CLARE

Before you leave the Portiuncula, may I lead you to the icon of Clare and myself outside the Portiuncula in Assisi? In a way this icon speaks of the invitation to healing, reconciliation and whole-ness that the hermitage experience enshrines. First I will tell you the beautiful story associated with this icon. Clare and I did not meet very often but on one occasion when we did meet we were clothed from on High with the love of God. This love for God, for each other and for all

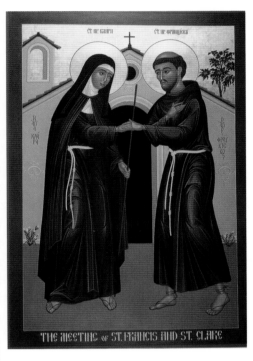

THE MEETING OF ST. FRANCIS AND ST. CLARE

our brothers and sisters and the whole of creation, so inflamed our hearts that it seemed to the people of Assisi that the valley was on fire. The good people of Assisi came running very fast to save the Portiuncula. When they arrived and saw that the fire was a divine fire, the fire of love, they were edified and consoled.

The icon then is a reminder to you of the divine love that leads to union and this union in love is all embracing, edifying and consoling. It happens on many levels of our being. With the eyes of your heart, look attentively and see the icon as a symbol of wholeness. It is the union of the masculine and the feminine not only between Clare and myself in the love of God, but it is also a union of the masculine and the feminine within Clare and within myself. Perhaps in your time in solitude you too may have entered more fully into the masculine and the feminine aspects within yourself.

I often referred to myself as a 'mother' who loves and cares for her children. I also liked to think of myself as a little hen protecting her chicks – just as Christ did when he walked on this earth. I also encouraged my brothers to have a 'mother-son' relationship, especially in the hermitage, so you see I was quite at home with my feminine side, eventually! *The Canticle of the Creatures*, which you have already prayed in the Chapel, reflects this union of the masculine and the feminine.

Note the gentleness, sensitivity, acceptance and union that this icon portrays. It is an image of you. As you continue your heart's journey, become 'mothers and fathers' in the image of God, whose likeness you bear. Go forth as bearers of life and love. It is in giving that we receive. Ultimately, you and I long for union. We long for union with others, within ourselves, and most of all, whether we recognize it or not, our deepest longing is for union with God, Father, Son and Holy Spirit. Embrace every opportunity for the mutual exchange of love that reflects the inner life of the Holy Trinity. Now let us pray together: Glory be to the Father, and to the Son and to the Holy Spirit, as it was in the beginning it now and ever shall be. World without end. Amen.

CLAY CROSS PORTIUNCULA

My dear brother, sister, friend and pilgrim, we have now come full circle and are at the open door at the entrance to the Portiuncula. When the time comes, you will leave your hermitage and return to God's beautiful world as his messenger of love, peace, goodness and joy. You will continue your journey to the hearts of others, seeking to nurture the goodness you find there, and holding the whole world in your heart with its pains and joys, anxieties and fears, hopes and dreams.

Until your next visit to your own sacred space of the

hermitage, the world will be your enclosure because I always told the brothers that unless we can live in peace within our own hearts, an outward enclosure is of no use. I ask God that he who is all-powerful, Three and One, bless all those who teach, learn, retain, remember, and put into practice all these things and may the Lord give you peace.

THE PEACE GARDEN

We have journeyed together within the Portiuncula, and we have talked about the world itself being your cloister, with this in mind let us walk outside to the Peace Garden. This garden captures something very special to me. Most people who know my story associate me with a love of creation. Yes, I did talk to birds and rabbits and lambs and crickets, wolves and worms, rocks and coloured flowers. And yes, I did compose my *Canticle of Creatures* calling the sun, the moon, the stars, water, wind and earth my sister, brother and mother. But I could do this only after my encounter with Jesus Christ, the First-born of all creation and the centre of all created reality. Then I understood as never before the wonder of creation in Christ Jesus, and how everything created, great and small, was a revelation of the lavish love and utter goodness of God. I will try to explain.

After my conversion, I walked through the world with the deepest reverence for everything that God has made. I was overwhelmed with the beauty and mystery of creation: how everything comes from God through Jesus Christ, and I felt impelled to love and reverence every creature as a gift from God in Christ, especially every human person, made in his image and likeness, but every individual created reality as well. I just wanted to praise, bless, love and adore him in and through all that he has made and to be in relationship with all and at peace with all.

Now in this twenty-first century I see signs of violence in creation because of the abuse and misuse of God's wonderful gift. This is why I am especially drawn to a Peace Garden where the gift of creation is treasured for what it really is: the manifestation of the infinite love and goodness of God. Of course St Paul has already said this in his Letter to the Colossians:

> He is the image of the unseen God
> and the first-born of all creation,
> for in Him were created
> all things in heaven and on earth.[80]

Be open to God's revelation of himself in and through creation. My friend, Saint Bonaventure, likened creation to a book. I think this is a very good symbol because we have to learn to read books and I would like to help you to read this beautiful book of creation. As we pray together in this Peace Garden let us be mindful of the words of my friend and brother, St Bonaventure:

> Whoever, therefore, is not enlightened
> by such splendour of created things
> is blind;
> whoever is not awakened by such outcries
> is deaf;

whoever does not praise God because of all these effects
is dumb;
whoever does not discover the First Principle
from such clear signs
is a fool.
Therefore, open your eyes,
alert the ears of your spirit, open your lips
and *apply your heart*
so that in all creatures you may
see, hear, praise, love and worship, glorify and honor
your God ...[81]

Understanding the book of creation will naturally draw you deeper into the wonder and beauty of the human person. At the beginning of my conversion, it was momentous for me to realize that because of what God did in Christ through the Incarnation, I have a relationship with every person and with the whole of creation. That is why I call each one my brother, my sister and my mother. This awareness led me to really see with the eyes of my heart the uniqueness that often lies hidden from us when we are too blind or too busy to see. Let me give you an example. In this Peace Garden there are trees, shrubs and flowers that are very obvious to see and many people admire them as trees, shrubs and flowers. Now I want you to look very carefully and reverently at a particular tree, a particular shrub or a particular flower. Notice that every leaf on the one tree is different from every other. Notice that the shrubs and flowers of a particular species are actually very different one from another even within that same species. How wonderful the richness and diversity of God's gift of creation. God never repeats himself.

When you begin to notice the book of creation, then you will be even more in awe when you see people with the eyes of your heart. Everyone and everything is made in the image of God, is from God and will return to God. Let us embrace this wonderful world of love and goodness and give thanks with hearts full of praise. We have already prayed my *Canticle of the Creatures* inside the Portiuncula. Now we can pray it again, and experience the peace that comes with being in union with God through all of his creation.

Most High, all-powerful, good Lord,
Yours are *the praises, the glory, and the honour, and all blessing,*
To You alone, Most High, do they belong,
And no human is worthy to mention Your name.
Praised be You, my *Lord*, with all *Your creatures,*

especially Sir Brother Sun,
Who is the day and through whom You give us light.
And he is beautiful and radiant with great splendour;
and bears a likeness of You, Most High One.

Praised be You, my Lord, through *Sister Moon and the stars*
in heaven you formed them clear and precious and beautiful.

Praised be You, my Lord, through Brother Wind,
and through the air, cloudy and serene, and every
    kind of weather,
through whom You give sustenance to Your creatures.

Praised be You, my Lord, through Sister *Water*
Who is very useful and humble and precious and chaste.

Praised be You, my Lord, through Brother *Fire,*
through whom *You light the night,*
and he is beautiful and playful and robust and strong.

Praised be You, my Lord, through our Sister Mother *Earth,*
who sustains and governs us, and who produces various *fruit*
with coloured flowers and *herbs.*

Praised be You, my Lord, through those who give pardon for Your love, and bear infirmity and tribulation. Blessed are those who endure in peace for by You alone Most High, shall they be crowned.

Praised be You, my Lord, through our Sister
Bodily Death, from whom no one living can escape.
   Woe to those who die in mortal sin.
Blessed are those whom death will find in Your
   most holy will for the second death shall do them no harm.
Praise and bless my Lord and give Him thanks and serve
Him with great humility.[82]

The Peace Garden enables you to ponder and praise God for the gift of creation and to become attentive to the peace and harmony that is yours to share. The symbols depicted here will give you the opportunity to reflect on the source and path to peace.

THE ARBOURS

There are two arbours at the entrance arch to this Peace Garden. One recalls an event from the life of my dear friend, St Clare and the other recalls a story from my own life. Both events are significant on the journey to peace, unity, healing and wholeness. Let me introduce you to Clare and she can speak for herself.

THE ARBOUR OF ST CLARE

I am Clare, daughter of Ortulana and Favorone of the Offreduccio family in Assisi. In God's divine providence, Francis and I were destined to live at the same time, in the same place and to share the same gospel path to God that remains vibrant to this day. I am pleased that I stand with St Francis at the entrance to this Peace Garden. And with Francis I now pray: May the Lord give you peace.

For now, I wish simply to retell an event that has a timeless message about the love and presence of God-with-us as our way to peace. I hope and pray that this story will strengthen your faith in the Eucharist as the source of peace and give you reassurance in your times of need and distress.

The year was 1240. Assisi was under siege from the troops

of Frederick II. Our monastery became a prime target and the troops scaled the walls of San Damiano and actually entered part of the cloister. My sisters were terrified in the face of such danger. I had been bedridden for six years and was very weak at this time but the sisters turned to me and I turned to the Lord. Fixing my thoughts on Jesus in the Holy Eucharist and mindful of his life-giving presence and self-giving love, I felt impelled to offer myself in union with his self-giving love for the sake of my sisters. I calmed and reassured them saying: My sisters and daughters, do not be afraid, because, if the Lord is with us, the enemy cannot harm us. Have confidence in our Lord Jesus Christ because he will free us. I want to be your hostage so that you do not do anything bad. If they come, place me before them.

It was a daring act, I know, but love is like that. It risks all. With great faith and confidence, I asked that the Blessed Sacrament be brought to me and I requested the sisters to take me to the door of our refectory, then with the Blessed Sacrament before me, I prostrated myself on the ground and in tears, cried from my heart: Lord, look upon these servants of yours, for I cannot protect them. Then a most wonderful thing happened and the sisters around witnessed that God's power is greatest in weakness. The two sisters who were holding me on either side also heard the voice of the Lord saying: 'I will always defend you.' Feeling such consolation and assurance, I then prayed for the whole of Assisi and said: Lord, be pleased also to defend this city, and the same sweet voice answered: 'The city will suffer many dangers but will be defended.' With that the hostile forces fled. They departed without harming or touching any one of us.

Our Eucharistic Lord protected and defended us that day and our hearts overflowed with thanksgiving and joy. And now I am here again among you reminding you of the infinite and humble love of Jesus in the Eucharist and the power of Eucharistic prayer on behalf of oneself, others and indeed of entire cities. Turn to him often. Tell him your fears and difficulties and dangers and listen to his voice in the depths of your heart. Jesus desires to share his gift of peace with you and the

Eucharist is the source of this peace. I often used to recall those words of St Francis where he emphasized the Eucharist as the source and the path to peace and reconciliation:

> I implore all of you brothers
> to show all possible reverence and honour
> to the most holy Body and Blood of our Lord Jesus Christ
> in whom that which is in heaven and on earth
> has been brought to peace and reconciled to almighty God.[83]

I would like to finish our brief conversation for now by giving you my blessing:

> I, Clare, a servant of Christ,
> a little plant of our most holy Father Francis,
> a sister and mother of you,
> although unworthy,
> beg our Lord Jesus Christ through his mercy
> and the intercession of His most holy Mother Mary
> and Blessed Michael the Archangel and all the holy angels of God,
> of our blessed father Francis, and all the men and women Saints,
> that the heavenly Father give you and confirm for you
> this most holy blessing *in heaven* and *on earth*. (cf. Gen. 27:28).
> On earth, may He multiply you in His grace and His virtues
> among His servants and handmaids in His Church Militant.
> In heaven, may He exalt you and glorify you
> among his men and women saints in His Church Triumphant. . . .
> May you always be eager to observe what you have promised the Lord.
> May the Lord always be *with you* . . .
> and may you always be with Him. Amen[84]

THE ARBOUR OF ST FRANCIS

Now it is my turn once again to share with you an event from my life that focuses on peace and peace making. You may have heard or read about this event which is commonly known as the story of the Wolf of Gubbio.[85] The people of this small town were terrified of a large and ravenous wolf that had frequented the vicinity and killed not only the

animals but some people as well. Fear and anxiety seized every household to the extent that they were afraid to venture outside the city gate. I took this opportunity to proclaim the message of Gospel peace not only to the wolf but also especially to the people. It was a wonderful opportunity for me to draw attention to truths that we can often ignore. Let me explain.

The wolf was really a great threat to the citizens of Gubbio. Yet I felt a deep compassion not only for the people but for the wolf as well! Now that may seem a strange thing to say but it is true. Suddenly I was intensely aware of the ravages of sin and the way in which it infiltrated every aspect of life with suspicion, hate, aggression, terror and violence. I shuddered at the thought of my own past skirmishes in battle but just as quickly I rejoiced in the remembrance of the love and good-ness of God. It was at that moment that I made a decision. The decision was for peace.

I told the people of Gubbio that I wanted to meet the wolf. At first they did not really believe me. They feared for my life just as they feared for their own lives and those of their fami-lies, flocks and herds, but I was determined. Without the protection of any armour and without weapons, I put my hope in the Lord and in the power of his Cross. Remembering the words of sacred Scripture that the Lord protects those who have confidence in him and will empower them to trample not only the wolf but also even the lion and the dragon, I set off.[86]

It was not long before I saw the terrifying wolf, jaws open, galloping towards me. Momentarily, I was transfixed. Then I made the Sign of the Cross and the wolf stopped in his tracks. I then called to the wolf as a brother. I actually remember what I said: 'Come here, brother wolf. On behalf of Christ I order you not to harm me or anyone else.' An amazing thing happened. The wolf closed his jaws, bowed his head and just lay there. This was my opportunity to announce peace. First I addressed the wolf – but always as a brother – and I reminded him of the way in which he had terrorized and violently killed in Gubbio and the surrounding area. But I tenderly assured Brother Wolf that peace was not only desirable but also possible for him and the people of Gubbio. I said many things to him, which he seemed to understand because at the end he gestured with his whole body that he too wanted peace. Of course I still had to make the people of Gubbio understand. You see, when people have been hurt and continue hurting, it takes a lot of courage to let go of resentments and fears, to forgive and to build up trust again. But it was worth a try. I decided to walk peacefully with the wolf into the town square. There I would take my God-given opportunity to proclaim the message of peace.

Seeing Brother Wolf and myself walking towards the square, the people followed, timidly at first, but then with great curiosity, relief and amazement, they followed – men, women and children. This was my longed-for moment. I started by saying: 'My very dear friends, return to the Lord and do worthy penance, and the Lord will free you now from the wolf, and in the future from the fires of hell.' I went on and on, explaining to the people that the wolf is a symbol of the anger, aggression and violence that lives within our own hearts. Of that we must repent. God desires that we live in peace, with him, with each other, within ourselves and with the whole of creation. I said many things that day because I knew from my own experience the struggle that is involved in facing the 'wolf' within oneself. The fear, anger, resentment, aggression, and violence that develop over the years, are often either projected onto the 'wolf' out there, or such feelings are walled in or walled out from the meeting and embrace that is required. It is in truth a naming and a taming process!

Therefore, dear friend, do not be afraid to look within your own heart. There, at the deepest level you will find the image of God within you. There you will find love and tenderness, goodness and beauty. But there too you may find that the image of God within has been deformed by sin and selfishness. The invitation and challenge to change your heart and your life is a gift from God to you. If you respond to his healing love and embrace your brokenness and poverty, he will be your healing and your riches. This is your moment! You will experience the joy of right relationships with God, with others and with the whole of creation. This leads to the fullness of life. This is peace. Let us spend some time in quiet prayer and then with great sorrow for all that is not at peace and with a great desire to be a channel of peace, let us pray together the *Peace Prayer*.

Lord,
Make me an instrument of your peace.
where there is hatred, let me sow love;
where there is injury, let me sow pardon;
where there is doubt, let me sow faith;
where there is despair, let me sow hope;
where there is darkness, let me sow light
and where there is sadness, let me sow joy.

THE LABYRINTH

On the journey to peace there are many helps along the way. The labyrinth is one such help and the very way in which it is constructed is symbolic of a journey. In other words, you walk step by step on the labyrinth, following the path through all the twists and turns until you arrive at the centre. I will tell you a little about this Christian practice and the symbolism it embodies, then perhaps you may decide to make the journey and open your heart to the message and meaning it may have for you.

In the Middle Ages when travel was not as easy as it is now, the practice of walking the labyrinth in the Cathedral was a popular one for those people who could not make pilgrimages to far off places such as The Holy Land or other shrines of Our Lady and the Saints. Therefore, the labyrinth was walked as a pilgrim with special intentions of intercession or thanksgiving. Others used the labyrinth to accompany Christ through the mysteries of his life on earth, especially his painful way to Calvary. Whatever the reason for walking the labyrinth, whether for oneself or others, it was and continues to be a sacred walk to draw people closer to God, deepening their relationship with him through his love and healing grace.

The labyrinth here in this Peace Garden is built on the model of the thirteenth-century labyrinth in Chartres Cathedral, France. It is circular in shape and has only one path that meanders through various alternating clockwise and anti-clockwise directions leading to the centre. The same path is then traversed back to where you started. The shape of the Cross of Christ is inbuilt within the total structure because of the central place of the cross in the Christian tradition, revealing the unconditional and total love of God for us. It is also a reminder that the cross touches your life too, interwoven as it is in the daily sufferings and limitations of your humanity. The six-petalled rose at the centre is a symbol for Mary, the Mother of God. One of the titles given to Mary by Christians is *Rosa Mystica*, which means Mystical Rose. It is Mary who waits for you at the centre to lead you to her son Jesus Christ, who is the centre of the Blessed Trinity, the centre of all created reality and the centre of the human person. allow Mary to mother Christ within you that he may be born anew within your heart and in your life. I repeat a similar message that I gave many years ago to the Brothers and Sisters of Penance.

> You will become a mother to Him when you carry Him in your heart and body through divine love and by a pure and sincere conscience. You will give birth to Him by your good works, which should shine as an example for others.[87]

Therefore, rest in his presence, listen to his word, and be open to his revelation of love. Our Lord Jesus Christ wishes to make his home and dwelling place with you.

The labyrinth may be walked many times and for many different reasons and intentions. However, there is a threefold movement within the structure of the labyrinth: there is the entering in and walking to the centre, there is the resting in the centre, and there is the walking out from the centre. This threefold path of cleansing, enlightenment and union is a familiar one to many Christians in their relationship with God. It has been described as The Three Ways. My dear brother, St Bonaventure, wrote a whole treatise called *Love Enkindled* in which he shows us how to grow stronger in our love for God through purification, enlightenment and deepening union. I like this emphasis on love and the enkindling of love through the spiritual helps that are available on the journey to God.

Now, perhaps you may wish to spend a little time in quiet preparation and prayer before entering the labyrinth. When you feel ready, we will pray together before you walk your pilgrim path.

PRAYER BEFORE WALKING THE LABYRINTH

Tender, loving God,
I thank you for this labyrinthine walk that I am about to make in
your presence.
May the single path that I will travel be a symbol of the true path
that leads to you.
Keep me on this path Lord, through the many twists and turns of
my life's journey.
As I approach the centre
may I come to a deeper awareness that you alone are the true
centre of my life.
Help me to rejoice in the wonder and mystery of your ways, Lord,
and in the return from the centre
may my life be centred on you
living through love in your presence. Amen.

As you journey, I would like to entrust you to Mary our Mother, reassuring you in the words of St Bernard of Clairvaux:

When you follow Her you cannot take a wrong turning;
when you pray to Her, you cannot lose hope;
when she fills your thoughts, you are sheltered from all error;
when she holds you up, you cannot fall;
when she protects you, you are never afraid;
when she leads you forward, you are never tired;
when her grace shines on you, you arrive at your goal.[88]

METHODS OF WALKING THE LABYRINTH

WALK TO ENKINDLE LOVE

From my own experience, I know that it is possible to be both spiritually blind and spiritually deaf to the Word of God. Therefore, the stage of purgation or cleansing of which St Bonaventure speaks will encourage you to cleanse your heart for Love's sake, of all that keeps you from the enjoyment of God in your life. You were made for the contemplation of God. May your sacred meditative walk help you to let go of all that holds you back from the fullness of life and love with God. If you seek with all your heart, in simplicity and humility, God will grant you his grace and you will be empowered to face whatever needs to be faced, to let go of whatever needs to be let go, to forgive whatever needs to be forgiven, and to give space to God. Giving God space becomes more evident as you reach the centre.

The centre is symbolic of the enkindling of love through enlightenment. Remain in the presence of God in the centre for as long as you feel the call to pray and meditate. You may see your life, or some aspect of your life in a different way — a personal relationship, a family situation, a working situation, a choice, a sickness — all can be seen through the eyes of Christ. But it takes time and silence to hear the Word of God within your heart. Be patient. Be open to love.

At the end of your time in the centre, begin the walk out. This is the stage of union and integration. You may feel the healing and empowerment of God's love and the desire for greater intimacy with him. You may also experience the desire to witness to that love by word and example in the days ahead. You may also feel able to embrace some aspect of yourself or your life that until now you were unable to face or accept. Every person is unique, therefore the experiences on the sacred walk of the labyrinth will also be unique expressions of the intimate and personal relationship every person has with God, Father, Son, and Holy Spirit.

WALK WITH ANGELS

I love angels. I was particularly devoted to the great archangels, especially St Michael. My special devotion to St Michael stemmed from the fact that he has the office of presenting souls to God. He is the one who opposed Satan and conquered evil and defeated those who rebelled against God. I used to spend forty days on Mount La Verna preparing for his special feast day, which he shares with the archangels, St Gabriel and St Raphael. Now let me invite you to walk with these three powerful intercessors with God.

Angels are known by proper names to indicate their powers and their work. As you prepare to enter the labyrinth, picture St Michael the archangel waiting for you at the entrance. The name Michael means 'Who is like God'. He it is who will lead you to know and love God as the one, true God, before whom no one and no thing can compare. Allow St Michael to help you to let go of all the false gods and idols that fill your life. With St Michael let your whole being adore God who is the Way, the Truth and the Life. Bow down in humble and joyful adoration as your heart expands with love and praise, and repent of the ways in which you may have sometimes misplaced your power to love. Thank St Michael for leading you to the centre of the labyrinth and especially to the centre of your own being where God dwells.

Now in the centre St Gabriel, the archangel is waiting to greet you. The name Gabriel means 'The Strength of God'. Gabriel's task is to announce. Here in the centre of the labyrinth, in the embrace of Mary, allow yourself to hear the Word of God announced to you. Accept that Word like Mary and know that with God all things are possible. St Gabriel told Mary not to be afraid. He speaks this message to you too. Without fear, and in peace be attentive to the Word of God. St Gabriel will help you to hear God's personal message for you. When you are ready St Gabriel will introduce you to your angel companion for the journey out.

As you prepare to leave the centre, the archangel Raphael is waiting to escort you. His name means 'Healing of God'. In Raphael's company you will experience joy and happiness because he brings to you the healing of God. Healing happens in many different ways – not always as we expect it to happen – but it does happen if we are open to it. Your need for healing may be spiritual, emotional, moral, physical – whatever your need, open yourself to the healing presence of God and with St Raphael give praise to God for his loving goodness and healing power.

WALK OF INNER SILENCE

You may wish to walk the labyrinth in silence, attentive to whatever the Holy Spirit may inspire within your heart. Simply open your heart to God and walk.

WALK OF THE JESUS PRAYER

If it helps, you may wish to repeat a short prayer, like the Jesus Prayer:

> Jesus Christ, Son of God, be merciful to me a sinner.

Or you may wish simply to repeat the holy name of Jesus.

WALK WITH SACRED SCRIPTURE

There are many Scripture verses that invite you to reflect on the theme of the path and as you are going to walk the sacred path of the labyrinth, you may wish to pray one or more of the following as you walk:

> You will reveal the path of life to me. (Ps. 16:8)

> I have treasured the words from your lips;
> in the path prescribed walking deliberately in your footsteps,
> so that my feet do not slip. (Ps.17:4)

> He guides me by paths of virtue for the sake of his Name.
> (Ps. 23:3)

> Lord, teach me your way, lead me in the path of integrity.
> (Ps. 27:11)

> Guide me in the path of your commandments, since my delight is
> there. (Ps. 119:35)

Now your word is a lamp to my feet, a light to my path.
(Ps. 119:105)

You know my path. (Ps. 142:3)

You will understand what virtue is ... All paths that lead to
happiness. (Pr. 2:9)

The path of the virtuous is like the light of dawn. (Pr. 4:18)

Come, that he may teach us his ways. (Is. 2:3)

The Lord says this: Put yourselves on the ways of long ago,
enquire about the ancient paths: which was the good way? Take it
then, and you shall find rest. (Jr. 6:16)

Prepare a way for the Lord, make his paths straight. (Mt. 3:3)

Hold up your limp arms and steady your trembling knees, and
smooth out the path you tread; then the injured limb will not be
wrenched, it will grow strong again. (Heb. 12:13)

Whatever Word of God you choose to pray as you walk the
labyrinth, give yourself space and time to savour it as God's
personal Word for you.

WALK OF PRAISE AND THANKSGIVING

Another way the sacred path may be used is to prayerfully and
reflectively give thanks and praise to God for the wonder of
your being and the gift of your unique creation. You are an image
of God in this world, chosen by God from all eternity, called by
name and given your own special vocation in life. By retracing
the story of your life as you meditate on the happy times and the
sad times, the big events and the small events, the challenges and
the changes, the successes and the failures, perhaps you will be
gently invited to embrace your life in its totality. All of it is part
of the person you are now, and just as you cannot skip over any

part of the labyrinthine path, so too with the journey of your life. The labyrinth is the place of laughter and tears, joy and sorrow, repentance and renewal but it is an all-embracing sacred space in which God invites you to receive healing and wholeness, to praise and to give thanks.

WALK FOR OTHERS

You may wish to call to mind a person for whom you wish to pray. Walk each step prayerfully for that special person and entrust him or her to the infinite love and care of God.

THE ROSARY WALK

Just as you retrace the steps and stages of your own life, you may also wish to walk with Jesus on his earthly journey. One way of doing this may be to pray your Rosary[89] and with Mary walk through the Joyful, Luminous, Sorrowful and Glorious mysteries in the life of Christ. You may also unite the mysteries of your own life with those of Jesus and Mary.

THE JOYFUL MYSTERIES

THE ANNUNCIATION

In the sixth month the angel Gabriel was sent by God to a town in Galilee called Nazareth, to a virgin betrothed to a man named Joseph, of the House of David; and the virgin's name was Mary. He went in and said to her, 'Rejoice, so highly favoured! The Lord is with you.' She was deeply disturbed by these words and asked herself what this greeting could mean, but the angel said to her, 'Mary, do not be afraid; you have won God's favour. Look! You are to conceive and bear a son, and you must name him Jesus ...' Mary said to the angel, 'But how can this come about, since I have no knowledge of man?' The angel answered, 'The Holy Spirit will come upon you, and the power of the Most High will cover you with its shadow. And so the child will be holy and will be called Son of God. And I tell you this too: your cousin Elizabeth also, in her old age, has conceived a son . . . for nothing is impossible to God.' Mary said, 'You see before you the Lord's servant, let it happen to me as you have said.' And the angel left her. (Lk. 1:26–38)

THE VISITATION

Mary set out at that time and went as quickly as she could into the hill country to a town in Judah. She went into Zechariah's house and greeted Elizabeth. Now it happened that as soon as Elizabeth heard Mary's greeting, the child leapt in her womb and Elizabeth was filled with the Holy Spirit. She gave a loud cry and said, 'Of all women you are the most blessed, and blessed is the fruit of your womb.' (Lk. 1:39–42)

THE BIRTH OF OUR LORD

So Joseph set out from the town of Nazareth in Galilee for Judea, to David's town called Bethlehem, since he was of David's House and line, in order to be registered together with Mary, his betrothed, who was with child. Now it happened that, while they were there, the time came for her to have her child, and she gave birth to a son, her first-born. She wrapped him in swaddling clothes, and laid him in a manger because there was no room for them at the living-space. (Lk. 2:4–7)

THE PRESENTATION IN THE TEMPLE

And when the day came for them to be purified in keeping with the Law of Moses, they took him up to Jerusalem to present him to the Lord ... Simeon blessed them and said to Mary his mother, 'Look, he is destined for the fall and for the rise of many in Israel, destined to be a sign that is opposed – and a sword will pierce your soul too – so that the secret thoughts of many may be laid bare.' (Lk. 2:22,34–35)

THE FINDING OF THE BOY JESUS IN THE TEMPLE

Every year his parents used to go to Jerusalem for the feast of the Passover. When he was twelve years old, they went up for the feast as usual. When the days of the feast were over and they set off home, the boy Jesus stayed behind in Jerusalem without his parents knowing it. They assumed he was somewhere in the party, and it was only after a day's journey that they went to look for him among their relations and acquaintances. When they failed to find him they went back to Jerusalem looking for him everywhere.

It happened that, three days later, they found him in the Temple, sitting among the teachers, listening to them, and asking them questions; and all those who heard him were astounded at his intelligence and his replies. They were overcome when they saw him, and his mother said to him, 'My child, why have you done this to us? See how worried your father and I have been, looking for you.' He replied, 'Why were you looking for me? Did you not know that I must be in my Father's house?' But they did not understand what he meant. (Lk. 2:41–50)

THE LUMINOUS MYSTERIES

THE BAPTISM OF JESUS

It was at this time that Jesus came from Nazareth in Galilee and was baptised in the Jordan by John. And at once, as he was coming up out of the water, he saw the heavens torn apart and the Spirit, like a dove, descending on him. And a voice came from heaven, 'You are my Son, the Beloved; my favour rests on you.' (Mk. 1:9–11)

THE MANIFESTATION OF JESUS AT CANA

On the third day there was a wedding at Cana in Galilee. The mother of Jesus was there, and Jesus and his disciples had also been invited. And they ran out of wine, since the wine provided for the feast had all been used, and the mother of Jesus said to him, 'They have no wine.' Jesus said, 'Woman, what do you want from me? My hour has not come yet.' His mother said to the servants, *'Do whatever he tells you.'* (Jn. 2:1–5)

THE PROCLAMATION OF THE KINGDOM AND THE CALL TO CONVERSION

After John had been arrested, Jesus went into Galilee. There he proclaimed the gospel from God saying, 'The time is fulfilled, and the Kingdom of God is close at hand. Repent, and believe the gospel.' (Mk. 1:14–15)

THE TRANSFIGURATION

Six days later, Jesus took with him Peter and James and John and led them up a high mountain where they could be on their own by themselves. There in their presence he was transfigured: his clothes became brilliantly white, whiter than any earthly bleacher could make them. Elijah appeared to them with Moses; and they were talking to Jesus. Then Peter spoke to Jesus: 'Rabbi,' he said, 'it is wonderful for us to be here; so let us make three shelters, one for you, one for Moses and one for Elijah.' He did not know what to say; they were so frightened. And a cloud came, covering them in shadow; and from the cloud there came a voice, 'This is my Son, the Beloved. Listen to him'. (Mk. 9:2–7)

THE INSTITUTION OF THE HOLY EUCHARIST

When evening came he arrived with the Twelve . . . And as they were eating he took bread, and when he had said the blessing he broke it and gave it to them. 'Take it,' he said, 'this is my body.' Then he took a cup, and when he had given thanks he handed it to them, and all drank from it, and he said to them, 'This is my blood, the blood of the covenant, poured out for many . . .' (Mk. 14:17,22–25)

THE SORROWFUL MYSTERIES

THE AGONY OF OUR LORD IN THE GARDEN

They came to a plot of land called Gethsemane, and he said to his disciples, 'Stay here while I pray.' Then he took Peter and James and John with him. And he began to feel terror and anguish. And he said to them, 'My soul is sorrowful to the point of death. Wait here, and stay awake.' And going on a little further he threw himself on the ground and prayed that, if it were possible, this hour might pass him by. 'Abba, Father!' he said, 'For you everything is possible. Take this cup away from me. But let it be as you, not I, would have it.' (Mk. 14:32–36)

THE SCOURGING AT THE PILLAR

Pilate anxious to placate the crowd, released Barabbas for them and, having ordered Jesus to be scourged, handed him over to be crucified. (Mk. 15:15)

THE CROWNING WITH THORNS

The soldiers led him away to the inner part of the palace, that is, the Praetorium and called the whole cohort together. They dressed him up in purple, twisted some thorns into a crown and put it on him. And they began saluting him, 'Hail, king of the Jews!' They struck his head with a reed and spat on him; and they went down on their knees to do him homage. And when they had finished making fun of him, they took off the purple and dressed him in his own clothes. (Mk. 15:16–20)

THE CARRYING OF THE CROSS

They then took charge of Jesus, and carrying his own cross he went out of the city to the Place of the Skull, or as it was in Hebrew, Golgotha. (Jn. 19:17)

THE CRUCIFIXION

Near the cross of Jesus stood his mother and his mother's sister, Mary the wife of Clopas, and Mary of Magdala. Seeing his mother and the disciple whom he loved standing near her, Jesus said to his mother, 'Woman, this is your son.' Then to the disciple he said, 'This is your mother.' (Jn. 19:25–27)

THE GLORIOUS MYSTERIES

THE RESURRECTION

On the first day of the week, at the first sign of dawn, they went to the tomb with the spices they had prepared. They found that the stone had been rolled away from the tomb, but on entering they could not find the body of the Lord Jesus. As they stood there puzzled about this, two men in brilliant clothes suddenly appeared at their side. Terrified, the women bowed their heads to the ground. But the two said to them, 'Why look among the dead for someone who is alive? He is not here; he has risen. Remember what he told you when he was still in Galilee: that the Son of man was destined to be handed over into the power of sinful men and be crucified, and rise again on the third day.' And they remembered his words.

(Lk. 24:1–8)

THE ASCENSION

Then he took them out as far as the outskirts of Bethany, and raising his hands he blessed them. Now as he blessed them, he withdrew from them and was carried up to heaven. They worshipped him and then went back to Jerusalem full of joy; and they were continually in the Temple praising God.

(Lk. 24:50–51)

THE DESCENT OF THE HOLY SPIRIT

When Pentecost day came round, they had all met together, when suddenly there came from heaven a sound as of violent wind which filled the entire house in which they were sitting; and there appeared to them tongues of fire; these separated and came to rest on the head of each of them. They were all filled with the Holy Spirit, and began to speak foreign languages as the Spirit gave them power to express themselves. (Acts 2:1–4)

THE ASSUMPTION OF MARY INTO HEAVEN

You are the glory of Jerusalem!
You are the great pride of Israel!
You are the highest honour of our race! (Jdt. 15:10)

THE CORONATION OF OUR LADY AS QUEEN OF HEAVEN

Now a great sign appeared in heaven; a woman, adorned with the sun, standing on the moon, and with twelve stars on her head for a crown. (Rev. 12:1)

WALKING THE WAY OF THE CROSS

As well as the many ways of walking the labyrinth, you may also wish to walk the Way of the Cross following the traditional Stations in the Christian tradition made popular by St Leonard of Port Maurice, a dear and faithful brother within my spiritual family.

From the moment of my conversion, I was devoted to Jesus crucified. The mystery of suffering and love captivated my heart as I contemplated Jesus on the Cross. I could see there the infinite love and tenderness of a God who made himself so vulnerable that he endured the awful sufferings of the way that led him from the Praetorium of Pilate where he was condemned to death, through fourteen 'stations' culminating in the crucifixion on Mount Calvary. I invite you to make this journey with Jesus, pondering in your heart, the love of Jesus that led him to suffer and die for you. Allow the Word of God to dwell in your heart and I will also share with you some verses from my own *Office of The Passion* that I prayed every day. They too are words from sacred Scripture that I imagined would be on the lips of Jesus during his time of suffering.

THE FIRST STATION: JESUS IS CONDEMNED TO DEATH

Pilate said to them, 'What am I to do with Jesus who is called the Christ?' They all said, 'Let him be crucified!' He asked, 'But what harm has he done?' But they shouted all the louder, 'Let him be crucified!' (Matt. 27:22–23).

> God, the wicked have risen against me,
> the assembly of the powerful has sought my life;
> they have not placed you in their sight.
> You are my most Holy Father,
> my King and my God.
> Come to my aid,
> Lord, God of my salvation.[90]

THE SECOND STATION: JESUS RECEIVES HIS CROSS

Then they took charge of Jesus, and carrying his own cross he went out to the Place of the Skull or, as it is called in Hebrew, Golgotha (Jn. 19:17).

> My Holy Father, King of heaven and earth, do not leave me, for trouble is near and there is no one to help.[91]

THE THIRD STATION: JESUS FALLS THE FIRST TIME

Now the hour has come for the Son of man to be glorified. In all truth I tell you, unless a wheat grain falls into the earth and dies, it remains only a single grain; but if it dies it yields a rich harvest. (Jn. 12:23–24).

When my spirit failed me,
You knew my ways.[92]

THE FOURTH STATION: JESUS MEETS HIS MOTHER

As the child's father and mother were wondering at the things that were being said about him, Simeon blessed them and said to Mary his mother, 'Look he is destined for the fall and for the rise of many in Israel, destined to be a sign that is opposed – and a sword will pierce your soul too – so that the secret thoughts of many may be laid bare' (Lk. 2:33–35).

Holy Virgin Mary,
among the women born into the world,
there is no one like you.
Daughter and servant
of the most high and supreme King
and of the Father in heaven,
Mother of our most holy Lord Jesus Christ,
Spouse of the Holy Spirit,
Pray for us ...[93]

THE FIFTH STATION: SIMON OF CYRENE HELPS JESUS

As they were leading him away they seized on a man, Simon from Cyrene, who was coming in from the country, and made him shoulder the cross and carry it behind Jesus (Lk.23:26).

O all you who pass along the way,
look and see if there is any sorrow like my sorrow.[94]

THE SIXTH STATION: VERONICA WIPES THE FACE OF JESUS

He had no form or charm to attract us,
no beauty to win our hearts;
he was despised, the lowest of men,
a man of sorrows, familiar with
suffering, one from whom, as it were,
we averted our gaze, despised, for
whom we had no regard (Is. 53:2–3).

Hear me, Lord, because your mercy is kind
Look upon me according to the greatness of your mercies.
Do not turn your face from your child;
because I am afflicted, quickly hear me.[95]

THE SEVENTH STATION: JESUS FALLS THE SECOND TIME

For we are bowed down to the dust, and lie prone on the ground. Arise! Come to our help! Redeem us, as your faithful love demands (Ps. 44:25–26).

They led me into the dust of death; and added sorrow to my wounds.[96]

THE EIGHTH STATION: JESUS SPEAKS TO THE WOMEN OF JERUSALEM

Large numbers of people followed him, and women too, who mourned and lamented for him. But Jesus turned to them and said, 'Daughters of Jerusalem, do not weep for me; weep rather for yourselves and for your children' (Lk. 23:27–28).

Blessed be the Lord my God,
Who has become my protector and my refuge
on the day of distress.[97]

THE NINTH STATION: JESUS FALLS THE THIRD TIME

Numbed and utterly crushed,
I groan in distress of heart. (Ps. 38:8)

> I have borne abuse because of you
> and confusion covers my face.
> Come to my aid,
> Lord, God of my salvation.[98]

THE TENTH STATION: JESUS IS STRIPPED OF HIS GARMENTS

When the soldiers had finished crucifying Jesus, they took his clothing and divided it into four shares, one for each soldier. His undergarment was seamless, woven in one piece from neck to hem; so they said to one another, 'Instead of tearing it, let's throw dice to decide who is to have it.' In this way the words of Scripture were fulfilled: They divide my garments among them and cast lots for my clothes. That is what the soldiers did (Jn. 19:23–24).

> I will hope in the shadow of your wings
> until wickedness pass by.[99]

THE ELEVENTH STATION: JESUS IS NAILED TO THE CROSS

When they reached the place called The Skull, they crucified him there and the two criminals, one on his right, the other on his left. Jesus said, 'Father, forgive them; they do not know what they are doing' (Lk. 23:35).

> For your mercy is exalted even to the skies,
> and your truth even to the clouds.
> be exalted above the heavens, O God,
> and may your glory be over all the earth.[100]

THE TWELFTH STATION: JESUS DIES ON THE CROSS

It was now about the sixth hour and the sun's light failed, so that darkness came over the whole land until the ninth hour. The veil of the Sanctuary was torn right down the middle. Jesus cried out in a loud voice saying, 'Father, *into your hands I commit my spirit.*' With these words he breathed his last (Lk. 23:44–46).

> I will praise you among the peoples, O Lord,
> I will chant a psalm to you among the nations.[101]

THE THIRTEENTH STATION: JESUS IS TAKEN DOWN FROM THE CROSS

It was the Day of Preparation, and to prevent the bodies remaining on the cross during the Sabbath — since that Sabbath was a day of special solemnity — the Jews asked Pilate to have the legs broken and the bodies taken away. Consequently, the soldiers came and broke the legs of the first man who had been crucified with him and then of the other. When they came to Jesus, they saw he was already dead, and so instead of breaking his legs one of the soldiers pierced his side with a lance; and immediately there came out blood and water. This is the evidence of one who saw it — true evidence, and he knows that what he says is true — and he gives it so that you may believe as well (Jn. 19:31–35).

> Holy Father, you held my right hand
> led me with your counsel
> and have taken me up with glory.
>
> For what is there in heaven for me,
> and what do I want on earth besides you?[102]

THE FOURTEENTH STATION: JESUS IS LAID IN THE TOMB

After this, Joseph of Arimathaea, who was a disciple of Jesus – though a secret one because he was afraid of the Jews – asked Pilate to let him remove the body of Jesus. Pilate gave permission, so they came and took it away. Nicodemus came as well – the same one who had first come to Jesus at night-time – and he brought a mixture of myrrh and aloes, weighing about a hundred pounds. They took the body of Jesus and bound it in linen cloths with the spices, following the Jewish burial custom. At the place where he had been crucified there was a garden, and in this garden a new tomb in which no one had yet been buried. Since it was the Jewish Day of Preparation and the tomb was nearby, they laid Jesus there (Jn. 19:38–42).

I have slept and risen,
and my most holy Father has received me with glory.[103]

To end this prayer of The Way of the Cross let us pray together *The Praises to be Said At All the Hours*:

> *Holy, holy, holy Lord, God Almighty,*
> *Who is, and Who was, and Who is to come:*
> And *let us praise and glorify Him forever!*
> *O Lord our God, you are worthy to receive*
> praise, *glory and honour* and blessing.
> And *let us praise and glorify Him forever!*
> *The Lamb Who was slain is worthy to receive*
> *power and divinity, wisdom and strength,*
> *honour and glory and blessing.*
> And *let us praise and glorify Him forever!*
> Let us bless the Father and the Son with the Holy Spirit:
> And *let us praise and glorify Him forever!*
> *Bless the Lord, all you works of the Lord.*
> And let us praise and glorify Him forever!
> *Sing praise to our God, all you his servants*
> *and you who fear God, the small and the great.*
> And *let us praise and glorify Him forever!*
> *Let heaven and earth praise Him Who is glorious .*
> And *let us praise and glorify Him forever!*
> Every creature *in heaven, on earth and* under the earth;
> and in the sea and *those which are in it.*
> And *let us praise and glorify Him forever!*
> Glory to the Father and to the Son and to the Holy Spirit:
> And *let us praise and glorify Him forever!*
> As it was in the beginning, is now, and will be forever. Amen.
> And *let us praise and glorify Him forever!*[104]

THE FRANCIS FOUNTAIN

Water! Oh, how I love Sister Water, so useful, humble, precious and pure. At this humble fountain you are invited to accept the invitation of Jesus who passionately and lovingly cries out to you: 'If anyone is thirsty, let him come to me! Whoever drinks the water that I shall give will never be thirsty again: the water that I shall give will turn into a spring inside you, welling up to eternal life.'[105]

The living water that Jesus is offering you at this moment is the gift of the Spirit of love. This precious gift cannot be bought or merited. It is pure gift. All you have to do is to respond to the invitation to 'Come'. In the Book of Revelation we read: 'I am the Alpha and the Omega, the Beginning and the End. I will give water from the well of life free to anyone who is thirsty ... Come! Let everyone who listens answer, Come! Then let all who are thirsty come: all who want it may have the water of life, and have it free.'[106] Dear brother, dear sister, thirst for the Spirit of God, the giver of life that is the gift of God then come and drink deeply of his love.

I always told my brothers and sisters to desire above all to have the gift of the Holy Spirit at work within them. I now repeat this to you as you prayerfully reflect on the words of Jesus about his promise of living water, meaning of course, the precious gift of the Holy Spirit bubbling up within you. Ardently desire and thirst for such a wonderful gift and then ask this same Holy Spirit to help you to understand the many fragrant words in sacred Scripture that are addressed to you through the symbol and mystery of Sister Water.

Perhaps you may feel the need of the cleansing water of God's loving mercy, then be comforted by the words of the prophet Ezekiel: 'I shall pour clean water over you and you will be cleansed; I shall cleanse you of all your defilement and all idols'.[107] Perhaps you may feel the need of healing, then reflect on the vision of Ezekiel when he saw the wholesome and medicinal waters of the spring in the Temple.[108] Whatever your need and desire do not be afraid to voice them in this sacred place.

During my short life on earth Sister Water lovingly helped me to minister to my brothers and sisters. I vividly remember travelling a long distance to a hermitage in the mountains. A kind friend accompanied me on the journey but on the way he almost died of thirst. He urgently cried to me to pray to our kind and gracious Lord to relieve his distress. With great compassion of heart I prayed unceasingly until I sensed that my prayer was answered. And so it was. Christ brought forth water from a rock and human thirst was quenched by the amazing kindness of God in Christ. There was no flow of water in that place before and none was found afterwards. I tell you this story simply to remind you of the loving providence of our gracious God who now invites you to quench your thirst in the ocean of his love and share with him all that is in your heart.

Notice the doves at my feet. How these remind me of my beautiful experience in the hermitage that I personally named Fonte Columbo. I named it thus because of the doves that came to drink at the fountain near the hermitage. Water and Dove: Baptism and the Holy Spirit. Reflect on the gift of new life in the Holy Spirit that you received at the moment of Baptism. Perhaps you may wish to renew your baptismal promises and hear once again those amazing words from sacred Scripture: You are my Beloved. My favour rests on you.

REVISITING THE STIGMATA

During your time apart both Clare and I have spoken to you about your personal call to holiness. We have stressed the beauty of your unique and unrepeatable creation and the challenge involved in becoming the person you are called to be. Now it seems fitting to remind you of the part that solitude plays in your journey of conversion and transformation in Christ.

When I welcomed you to the La Verna hermitage I shared with you something of my experience there. Now in this Peace Garden, I have one final invitation and challenge as you reflect and meditate once again on this peak experience in my heart's journey. My friend, friar Bonaventure prayed and reflected on the process of conversion and transformation in my life and you may find his reflection helpful as you open your heart to love's purifying and transforming power.

> After true love of Christ
> *transformed* the lover *into His image,*
> when the forty days were over that he spent in solitude
> as he had desired,
> and the feast of St. Michael the Archangel
> had also arrived,
> the angelic man Francis
> *came down from the mountain*
> bearing with him
> the likeness of the Crucified,
> depicted not on tablets of stone or on panels of wood
> carved by hand,
> but engraved on parts of his flesh
> *by the finger of the living God.*[109]

Remain here for a while and reflect on what the finger of the living God desires to engrave on your heart that you may resemble him more fully. Become more deeply aware that 'your heart is the altar of God. It is here that the fire of intense love must burn always.'[110] But remember, it is love and love alone that transforms us into his image. Open your heart to love.

MOTHER OF PEACE

Now before you leave the Peace Garden, spend time with Mary, Mother of Jesus and your Mother. She longs for you to experience the gift of peace promised by her son, Jesus. Don't hurry your visit with your Mother. Notice how she looks at you and with outstretched hand longs to draw you to her heart. Place all your worries, fears, desires, dreams and intentions in her outstretched hand. In your heart and in your conversation with Mary your Mother, place all those you love and care for in her loving, tender, motherly embrace. Allow her to take them to her heart and to the heart of her Son. She will speak to Jesus for you. Do not be afraid. Have confidence and be at peace.

As you continue your heart's journey, take time and make space to nurture the gift of peace, which is God's gift to you and recall often those beautiful words of the risen Jesus:

> Peace be with you.
> As the Father sent me,
> so I am sending you. (Jn. 20:21)

Yes, our vocation is never just for ourselves. Ours is the privilege of reaching out to the hearts of our brothers and sisters and to the whole of creation in all-embracing and unconditional love.

> May the Lord give you peace.

NOTES

1. Armstrong *et al., Francis of Assisi*, vol. 1, p. 201.
2. Gn. 24:60.
3. Gn. 4:7.
4. Psalms 107, 118.
5. Is. 38:10.
6. Mt. 16:18.
7. Ps. 118.
8. Lk. 24.
9. Jn. 14:6.
10. Pr. 3; Ps. 119.
11. Jn. 8:12.
12. Adm. 5:1.
13. Armstrong *et al., Francis of Assisi*, vol. 1, pp. 124–5.
14. 1 P. 2:4.
15. Ps. 18:2.
16. Eph. 2:20–22.
17. Armstrong *et al., Francis of Assisi*, vol. 2, p. 596.
18. Hos. 2:16.
19. Sg. 5:4.
20. Armstrong *et al., Francis of Assisi*, vol. 1, p. 46.
21. Armstrong *et al., Francis of Assisi,* vol. 2, p. 542.
22. Armstrong *et al., Francis of Assisi*, vol. 2, p. 374.
23. Armstrong *et al., Francis of Assisi*, vol. 1, p. 163.
24. Armstrong *et al., Francis of Assisi*, vol. 1, p. 83.
25. Armstrong *et al., Francis of Assisi*, vol. 1, p. 518.
26. Armstrong *et al., Francis of Assisi*, vol. 1, pp. 81–2.
27. Armstrong *et al., Francis of Assisi*, vol. 1, p. 49.
28. Mt. 28:20.
29. Armstrong *et al., Francis of Assisi*, vol. 1, p. 118.
30. Ibid.
31. Ex. 3:1–6.
32. Ex. 13:21–2.
33. Lk. 12:49.

34. *Armstrong et al., Francis of Assisi* vol. 2, p. 686.
35. Armstrong *et al., Francis of Assisi*, vol. 1, p. 49.
36. Armstrong *et al., Francis of Assisi*, vol. 2, p. 316.
37. Armstrong *et al., Francis of Assisi*, vol. 1, p. 163.
38. Pope John Paul II, *Ecclesia De Eucharistia*, Numbers 54 & 55, pp. 30–1.
39. Armstrong *et al., Francis of Assisi*, vol. 1, pp.113–14.
40. Rv. 4:5.
41. Gn. 2:1–3.
42. Lk. 17:4.
43. Rv. 4:8.
44. Armstrong *et al., Francis of Assisi*, vol. 1, p. 162.
45. Armstrong *et al., Francis of Assisi*, vol. 1, pp. 61–2.
46. Lk. 10:38–42.
47. Jn. 10:10.
48. Rv. 1:8.
49. Jn. 4:1–41, 7:37–9.
50. Rv. 2:17.
51. Armstrong *et al., Francis of Assisi*, vol. 2, p. 386.
52. Armstrong *et al., Francis of Assisi*, vol. 1, p. 40.
53. Armstrong, Regis J., OFM, *Clare of Assisi Early Documents*, p. 48.
54. Armstrong, Regis J., *Clare of Assisi Early Documents*, p. 44.
55. Armstrong *et al., Francis of Assisi*, vol.1, p. 105.
56. Armstrong *et al., Francis of Assisi*, vol. 1, pp. 128–137.
57. Armstrong *et al., Francis of Assisi*, vol. 1, pp. 120–1.
58. Cf. Damien Vorreux, OFM., *A Franciscan Symbol. The Tau.*
59. Ez. 9: 4.
60. Armstrong *et al., Francis of Assisi*, vol. 1, p. 70.
61. Armstrong *et al., Francis of Assisi*, vol. 1, p.118.
62. Armstrong *et al., Francis of Assisi*, vol.1: pp. 253–5, 307, 397, 405–6, 526; vol. 2, pp. 174-5, 177, 227-8, 237, 269-70, 277, 287, 289, 355, 410, 412, 414, 592, 594, 610, 619, 706, 783; vol. 3, pp 104, 151, 232, 345, 558.
63. Armstrong *et al., Francis of Assisi*, vol. 1, p. 131.
64. Armstrong *et al., Francis of Assisi*, vol. 1, p. 205–7, vol. 2, p. 333.
65. Armstrong *et al., Francis of Assisi*, vol. 1, pp. 205–6.
66. Armstrong *et al., Francis of Assisi*, vol. 1, pp. 49–50.
67. Armstrong *et al., Francis of Assisi*, vol. 2, p. 67, 286, vol. 3, p. 505.
68. Armstrong *et al., Francis of Assisi*, vol. 2, p. 685.
69. Armstrong *et al., Francis of Assisi*, vol. 2, pp. 131, 171, 189, 196–7, 226, 276, 410–11, 416, 558, 634, 711; vol. 3, pp. 197, 232, 313, 359, 363, 416.

70. Armstrong et al., *Francis of Assisi*, vol. 1, p. 159.
71. Armstrong et al., *Francis of Assisi*, vol. 2, p. 190.
72. Jn. 6:63.
73. Armstrong et al., *Francis of Assisi*, vol. 1. p. 158.
74. Armstrong et al., *Francis of Assisi*, vol. 1, pp. 36, 39, 108, 176–7, 238, 242, 262–3, 404, 409–10, 526; vol. 2, pp. 108, 191, 226, 280, 402, 472–3, 498, 530, 593, 618, 630, 634, 701, 709, 711; vol. 3, pp. 141, 193, 318, 346, 365, 433–4, 452–5, 529, 560–1, 649, 652–3, 655–6, 667, 687, 801–3, 855, 866, 874.
75. 'Armstrong et al., *Francis of Assisi*, vol. 3, pp. 453–4.
76. Habig, *St. Francis of Assisi, Omnibus of Sources*, p. 1448.
77. 'Armstrong et al., *Francis of Assisi*, vol. 1, p. 109.
78. Armstrong et al., *Francis of Assisi*, vol. 1, p. 84.
79. Pope John Paul II, *Guardian of the Redeemer . Redemptoris Custos. Apostolic Exhortation*, Rome: The Vatican. Article 17, 1989.
80. Col. 1:15-20.
81. Bonaventure, *The Soul's Journey into God*, pp. 67–8.
82. Armstrong et al., *Francis of Assisi*, vol. 1. pp. 113–14.
83. Armstrong et al., *Francis of Assisi*, vol. 1, p. 117.
84. Armstrong, Regis J., OFM, *Clare of Assisi, Early Documents*, pp. 78–9.
85. Armstrong et al., *Francis of Assisi*, vol. 3, pp. 482–5.
86. Ps. 91:13.
87. Armstrong et al., *Francis of Assisi*, vol. 1, p. 42.
88. Artress, Lauren. *Walking a Sacred Path.* pp. 162–3.
89. The Rosary is a rhythmic and meditative prayer, conducive to nurturing a sense of peace as you keep pace with the repetition of the prayers and the walking. Each meditation consists of praying the Our Father once followed by praying the Hail Mary 10 times concluding with the Glory Be to the Father. During the recitation of these prayers, one mystery of the life of Christ is pondered. Rosary beads may be used for this prayer.
90. Armstrong et al., *Francis of Assisi*, vol. 1, p. 142, Ps. 1:5.
91. Ibid., p. 140, Ps. 1:5.
92. Ibid., p. 144, Ps. 5:3.
93. Ibid., p. 141.
94. Ibid., p. 146, Ps. 6:1.
95. Ibid., p. 153, Ps. 12:7–8.
96. Ibid., p. 146, Ps. 6:10.
97. Ibid., p. 153, Ps. 12:9.
98. Ibid., p. 145, Ps. 5:7, 16.
99. Ibid., p. 143, Ps. 3:2.
100. Ibid., p. 143, Ps. 3:11–12.

101. Ibid., p. 143.
102. Ibid., p. 146, Ps. 6:12–13.
103. Ibid., p. 146, Ps.6:11.
104. Armstrong *et al., Francis of Assisi*, vol. 1, p. 161
105. Jn. 7:37;4:13–14.
106. Rv. 21:6, 17.
107. Ez. 36:25–26.
108. Ez. 47:1–12.
109. Armstrong *et al., Francis of Assisi*, vol. 2, p. 634.
110. Bonaventure, *On the Perfection of Life*, p. 239.

BIBLIOGRAPHY

Armstrong, Regis J., OFMCap.; Hellmann, Wayne J.A., OFMConv.; Short, William J., OFM, *Francis of Assisi. The Saint. Early Documents*, vol. 1, London: New City Press, 2000.

Armstrong, Regis J., OFMCap.; Hellmann, Wayne J. A., OFMConv.; Short, William J., OFM, *Francis Of Assisi. The Founder. Early Documents*, vol. 2, London: New City Press, 2000.

Armstrong, Regis J., OFMCap.; Hellmann, Wayne J. A., OFMConv.; Short, William J. OFM, *Francis Of Assisi. The Prophet. Early Documents*, vol. 3. London: New City Press, 2001.

Armstrong, Regis J., OFMCap. (ed.), *Clare of Assisi. Early Documents*. New York: Paulist Press, 1988.

Artress, Lauren, Dr, *Walking a Sacred Path. Rediscovering the Labyrinth as a Spiritual Tool.* New York: Riverhead Books, 1995.

Bonaventure, Saint, 'On the Perfection of Life Addressed to Sisters' in *The Works of Bonaventure Seraphic Doctor and Saint. Mystical Opuscula*, translated from the Latin by Jose de Vinck, Paterson New Jersey: St Anthony Guild Press, 1960.

Bonaventure, *The Soul's Journey into God: The Tree of Life; The Life of St. Francis*, The Classics of Western Spirituality, Ewert Cousins (tr.), New York, Paulist Press, 1978.

Habig, Marion A. (ed.), *Saint Francis of Assisi, Writings and Early Biographies. English Omnibus of Sources for the Life of St. Francis*, USA: Franciscan Herald Press, 1983.

New Jerusalem Bible, London: Darton, Longman & Todd, 1994.

Vorreux, Damien, OFM, *A Franciscan Symbol, the Tau: History, Theology and Iconography*, Translation from the French by Marilyn Archer, OSF and Paul Lachance, OFM, Chicago, Illinois: Franciscan Herald Press, 1979.

Appendix

COPYRIGHT PERMISSIONS

Texts
Francis of Assisi, *Early Documents*, vols. I–III, New City.
The Jerusalem Bible, Darton, Longman & Todd Ltd.

Picture/Photo	Artist/Publisher/Address
Cover picture: St Francis	Sr Kay Berger, OSF The Canticle Studio 1550 Plainfield Road Joliet, Il. 60435
p. 3 St Francis	Giotto in Patriarchale Basilica Sacro Convento di San Francesco Assisi
p. 5 Francis and the Leper	Piero Casentini Via Colle Sant'Upica 25b Valmontone (Rm)
p. 8 The Path	Paul Ratigan Photo/Graphics Ltd www.paulratigan.co.uk
p. 12 The Sedum Roof	Paul Ratigan Photo/Graphics Ltd www.paulratigan.co.uk

p. 13 Our Lady of The Angels — Sister Mary Anthony Roberts, FSM
San Damiano Convent
Alfreton
Derbyshire

p. 24 Angels — Sister Mary Anthony Roberts, FSM

p. 25 Angels — Sister Mary Anthony Roberts, FSM

p. 26 The Contemplation Space — Paul Ratigan Photo/Graphics Ltd
www.paulratigan.co.uk

p. 31 The San Damiano Cross — Sister Mary Anthony Roberts, FSM

p. 37 The Hermitages — Paul Ratigan Photo/Graphics Ltd
www.paulratigan.co.uk

p. 41 St Francis receives the Stigmata — Giotto in Bardi Chapel, Church of Sante Croce, Florence

p. 51 Blessing for Brother Leo — Giotto in Patriarchale Basilica Sacro Convento di San Francesco Assisi

p. 53 Solitude in Fraternity — Paul Ratigan Photo/Graphics Ltd
www.paulratigan.co.uk

p. 54 Martha and Mary — National Galleries of Scotland
Picture Library
Scottish National Gallery of
Modern Art
75 Belford Road
Edinburgh EH4 3D

p. 56 The Holy Family — Sister Mary Anthony Roberts, FSM

p. 57 Francis and Clare — Robert Lentz
© 2008
Courtesy of Trinity Stores
www.trinitystores.com

p. 58 Clay Cross Portiuncula — Paul Ratigan Photo/Graphics Ltd
www.paulratigan.co.uk

p. 64 Brother Sun, Sister Moon — Poor Clare Monastery
Humbie, Edinburgh, Scotland.

p. 65 Brother Wind, Sister Water   Poor Clare Monastery
Humbie, Edinburgh, Scotland.

p. 66 Brother Fire   Poor Clare Monastery
Humbie, Edinburgh, Scotland

p. 67 Pardon   Sister Mariella Erdmann OSF
Franciscan Federation USA

p. 67 Sister Death   Basilica Sacro Convento di San
Francesco Assisi
www.sanfrancescoassisi.org

p. 68 Arbour of St Clare   Sister Mary Anthony Roberts, FSM

p. 71 Arbour of St Francis   Sister Mary Anthony Roberts, FSM